DATE DUE			

Looking Both Ways

Exploring the Interface Between Christianity and Sociology

Richard Perkins

BAKER BOOK HOUSE
Grand Rapids, Michigan 49516

261
P4lL
144130
May 1988

To my wife **Beaver:**

Who gives me the strength
to get up and do what has to be done

Contents

Preface

My graduate education in sociology was thoroughly secular. Even before completing my degree, I began teaching at a small Presbyterian college where "Christian emphasis" was limited to a prayer read before the first faculty meeting by the head (and only member) of the Religion Department. Even though I was a Christian and a sociologist, I fit in with the atmosphere of the college rather comfortably. I taught my students what I had been taught: "value-free sociology." I told my students that personal values had to be kept separate from scientific facts. "Bracket your values," I insisted. Most of them tried.

Teaching, however, is a continuing education in itself, and the attentive students lost little time in pointing out what I hadn't noticed—that my lectures were riddled with values and untestable assumptions. In fact, I began to notice that some of the values implied in my lectures were ones to which I did not wish to be personally committed. Apparently, value-free sociology left a lot to be desired.

By now I was teaching at a more emphatically religious college—one where the faculty sang hymns together (and could do so without hymnals), and someone other than the head of the Religion Department prayed before *every* faculty meeting.

9

What's more, the students at this school were interested in more than the so-called straight facts—often pressing me to give an account of how my Christian commitment squared with what I taught. Of course, I had little if any idea, but I began thinking more about it, and included these thoughts in my lectures.

That's how this book was written—through a long, drawn-out effort to give a more coherent account (to my students and to myself) of how Christianity relates to sociology and vice versa. In the beginning, as I've already said, I kept the two ways of thinking in separate compartments. Recognizing the inadequacy of this approach, I lurched to the opposite assumption— that is, that the fit between the two ways of thinking is perfect: no problems at all, only apparent ones that could be figured out with a little more clear thinking all around.

As I continued teaching, writing, reading, and talking to my students and other faculty members, however, I grew less assured. I had picked up an assumption popular among Christian academicians—something along the lines of "all truth is God's truth." To remain faithful to that assumption, I had to torture first one and then the other perspective in order to respond adequately to the problems that continued to surface. This *integrative* approach was as unsuccessful as the former *value-free* approach.

Consequently, ideas slowly changed in my mind. The result is that Christian sociology is no longer the neat system I once thought it would/should/could be. To some extent, far from meshing perfectly, the Christian and the sociological parts of my thinking continue to glare at each other from opposite corners of my mind.

These thoughts form the basis of my current thinking. The rest of my thoughts are still being typed into this manuscript because my trusty word processor allows continuous changes as they occur to me. However, when a manuscript becomes a published book, it is then picked up by you, the reader, and read as a completed project. Now it is an entity in itself—objective and finished—even though the thinking and the changes continue in the author's mind.

The title *Looking Both Ways* conveys several meanings. First, it carries a deliberate tone of warning. We remind ourselves to look both ways before stepping into a dangerous situation. Under these circumstances, looking both ways is an important precaution. The cautionary tone is deliberate; sociology and Christianity do not naturally get along, and something always has to give when the two are juxtaposed.

There is, however, another message in the title: the imperative to look both ways is also intended as an encouragement to understand the social world from several distinct perspectives simultaneously. Christians can benefit by learning what sociology has to offer, and vice versa.

I have tried to emphasize the second message over the first; I want the promise of what can be gained from the combination of sociology and Christianity to predominate over the warning. Even so, the warning remains an important message, one which is stressed in Part 1. The opportunity and promise of Christian sociology is emphasized more in the content of Part 2.

I write for Christians interested in sociology—primarily for undergraduates—but also for seminary students and ministers who want to know more about how Christian and sociological thought intersect. This book represents primarily a sociological rather than a theological effort; I assume that the reader knows more about Christianity than sociology. As a result, I will make a greater effort to spell out the elements of sociological thought than to discuss the elements of Christianity.

I have addressed some controversial issues in this book, so I anticipate objections raised against both its purpose and execution. No problem: my purpose here is to start an argument, not finish one.

I want to acknowledge first my intellectual indebtedness to Professor Peter Berger of Boston University. I am one of many students who first encountered the excitement of sociological analysis through Berger's lucid insights. Even though I do not always agree with his conclusions and even though he regards the purpose of books such as this with suspicion (if not alarm), I owe him a great deal. His influence will be evident throughout to those familiar with his writings.

Deans Fred Shannon and Jim Barnes generously provided funds covering the costs of typing, and Mary Boomhower, Diane Neal, and Rick Phillips conscientiously typed its early drafts. My wife Beaver also helped with the typing and proofreading. My thanks to them all.

Many colleagues have read one or more chapters, offering

many suggestions for improvement. I am indebted to David Basinger, Lionel Basney, Ron Burwell, Dick Christopherson, Ray DeVries, George Hillery, David Howard, Ken Inskeep, Winston Johnson, Mike Leming, Sherwood Lingenfelter, Herb Schlossberg, and Dawn Ward. Each provided valuable editorial assistance, raising questions in the process that caused me to rethink my ideas and my presentation. I didn't always comply with their recommendations, but I was challenged by them all to rethink what I had to say.

I especially want to thank my friend Brian Sayers. He used his considerable skills in philosophy to challenge my wilder assertions and to help me clarify my arguments. Without his help, this book would have been far less cogent and coherent than it is. More likely, it wouldn't even exist.

Richard Perkins
Houghton, New York

Introduction

Sociologists and Christians have a good deal to say to each other. Unfortunately, what is said is often not encouraging. On the one hand, many sociologists have rather strong biases against Christianity. One sociologist I know admitted that he had "stopped believing what I was taught by my Christian parents while I was in college." He added that he knew many sociologists who had similar experiences. He presumed that jettisoning one's faith was simply a part of growing into sociological maturity. He admitted, however, that he had never given Christianity a fair analysis, but that he intended to do so . . . someday.

Likewise, I have met many conservative Christians who have deep misgivings about sociology. In fact, I know several ministers who regularly warn their congregations against sending their children to liberal-arts colleges because, if the children enrolled in one, they might take a sociology course. Were this to happen, their faith would certainly be undermined, if not destroyed.

Christians are often unsettled by the tensions they sense and the contradictions they perceive between what they believe as Christians and what they learn from sociology. The form and the content of sociological analysis often appear hostile to orthodox

Christians. Sociologists are less likely than most other academics to be committed to a supernatural world view. They are therefore less likely than other professors to be sympathetic with students who assume that the spiritual and natural realms are equally real (Lehman, 1974).

I am both a Christian and a sociologist. Given my commitment to looking both ways, perhaps some readers will be surprised to learn that I think some of these mutual suspicions are warranted. A central purpose for this book, then, is to explore these reasons and to analyze what can be done about them, if anything. However, I am not trying to write defensively. This is not an effort to apologize to my sociological colleagues for my Christian commitments, or vice versa. Rather, I want to show why looking both ways is crucial to both perspectives. In other words, I would like to convince the reader that the lack of either perspective diminishes the other.

I believe that a substantial measure of good can come from a reasonable dialogue between Christian and sociological perspectives. My purpose, then, is to lay a sufficient groundwork so this type of dialogue can go forward.

Terms Associated with Sociology

Those who already know a good deal about the discipline will recognize various themes I have borrowed from diverse schools of sociological thought. There are, of course, important issues that divide one theoretical school from another, but I am convinced that there is merit in presenting an integrated theoretical approach. Of course, I have my own theoretical biases, and readers well versed in sociological theory will perceive a theoretical lean here and there. Even so, I have tried not to lean only in one direction.

Looking Both Ways is organized around two central sociological themes—themes which are not equally subscribed to by all sociologists. Both themes have direct bearing on the ways Christians and sociologists think about the social world. In Part 1, I examine the claim that social reality is socially constructed—the main premise to what is sometimes called "Constructionist (or interpretational) Sociology." In Part 2, I examine some of the traits of "Structuralist Sociology"—in particular, the claim that individuals are controlled by social structures (that is, roles, institutions) which shape biographical experience.

Now, *constructionist* and *structuralist* brands of sociology are in some ways quite incompatible, and I certainly do not want to leave the reader with the false impression that they combine to form a seamless theoretical web. Even so, these two ideas—(1) that social reality is a human construction; and (2) that humans are conditioned by the structures of social experience—are prevalent throughout the discipline. They tend to show up in one form or another in nearly every sociology course, particularly at the introductory level. Together, they form what Peter Berger (1963) calls "the paradox of social existence"—the seemingly contradictory assertions that society defines us, but is in turn defined by us.

Terms Associated with Christianity

Christian: Any person who identifies with and subscribes to the Christian gospel. This gospel, in its most rudimentary expression, consists of the following assertions:

1. A harmonious and balanced world came into existence through divine agency.
2. This creation has been thrown out of balance by humans.
3. Jesus, God's Son, has attempted to "set things right" through his life and death.
4. Living according to Jesus' example helps us to restore proper balance to the world.

A Christian, then, is an advocate of religion based on the life and teachings of Jesus—a person who endorses the qualities of his life and the message taught by him. This broad definition includes Roman Catholics and Southern Baptists, Seventh-Day Adventists and Pentecostals, and millions of others who call themselves Christians.

Orthodox Christians: persons committed to the historical doctrines of Christianity, including the virgin birth of Christ, his divinity, atoning death, and resurrection, the reality of eternal salvation and damnation, and the trinitarian nature of God.

Despite doctrinal differences that separate orthodox Christians into various theological camps, all are (for the purposes of this book at least), considered orthodox if they support these doctrines. (Other doctrines considered nonessential here include the authority of the Roman Catholic pope, the correct method of baptism, the proper order of church-state relations, and so forth.)

Evangelical Christians: At the doctrinal core, contemporary evangelicals are identified by their adherence to certain doctrinal beliefs.

1. The Bible is the authoritative and inspired Word of God.
2. Christ's life, death, and the physical resurrection is efficacious for the salvation of human souls.
3. Each Christian must make a personal decision, which results in conversion.
4. Jesus Christ will come again and judge all people as to their eternal status, and
5. All Christians have a commission to tell the unsaved world the gospel message.

Fundamentalist Christian: Theologically the same as the above position, except for a greater preference for dispensationalism, premillennialism, and the insistence that the Bible must be interpreted literally. In so doing, fundamentalists tend to downplay sociocultural influences on the interpretive process. In addition, fundamentalists are characterized by a greater emphasis on separation from various symbols of "the world," such as drinking alcohol, social dancing, and so forth.

The difference between evangelicals and fundamentalists is more a matter of style and emotional tone than theology, with the fundamentalists taking a more defensive, separatistic, and anti-intellectual stance. Someone once called evangelicals "polite fundamentalists." There is more than mere wit associated with this assertion.

As mentioned earlier the purpose of this book is twofold, corresponding to the two sections. To describe the focus another way, in Part 1, I will "think Christianly" about sociology. In Part 2, I will "think sociologically" about contemporary evangelical

Christianity. In short, I will examine the possibilities of and the problems associated with these two ways of looking at the social world.[1]

Those of us who teach at evangelical colleges and universities often talk about "the integration of faith and learning." I've never been less sure of what this phrase means than I am now. This book will reflect this uncertainty. For most sociologists, Christian sociology appears to be a contradiction in terms. Depending on how each term is defined, it very well could *be* a contradiction in terms. Yet this combination is exactly what I intend to explore—that is, the degree to which sociology and orthodox Christianity can speak critically to each other.

As we will see, the two perspectives do not usually try to sensitize and inform us on the same issues and in the same way. One factor: sociology represents an orientation that is "checkable" in ways that Christianity (or any other religion) is not. I will argue, however, that in some respects sociological thought is similarly uncheckable, and that this fact is the major reason why the phrase "Christian sociology" is something other than a simple contradiction in terms.

To clarify these points, I will comment further on the *purpose, type,* and *focus* of this effort.

The PURPOSE of Integrative Efforts

Christian sociology can have as many purposes as there are facets to the sociological enterprise. The phrase is sometimes used to refer to any sociological effort to study and thereby understand Christianity. Because social reality is symbolic, sociologists must understand the symbolic meanings of the people whose interaction they study. So, for example, if sociologists want to study a group of Christians, they must first comprehend

---

1. Of course, obvious limitations must be considered whenever religious beliefs are contrasted with scientific argument. For instance, biblical Christianity does not offer a complete basis for a sociological perspective. Problems of scriptural interpretation aside, the Bible is not a sociology textbook. It does not offer an empirically verifiable approach to explaining social reality, but it does offer insights into human nature and the nature of social organization—insights that transcend cultural limitations and societal circumstances. Even so, any effort to correspond modern philosophical and scientific perspectives with two-thousand-year-old writings will have to proceed with considerable caution and restraint.

Christian modes of thinking and acting. Since evangelicalism is an important religious movement in our sector of the world, it helps to have Christian sociologists available to pursue the study.

In addition to opening up avenues of research, Christian sociology can also alert sociologists to areas of study often neglected or misunderstood by other sociologists, especially those subjects of a so-called spiritual nature. Many forms of religious experience have been studied from a Christian perspective; the relationships between love, freedom, and communal solidarity (Hillery, 1981) and spiritual well-being (Moberg, 1979) have been researched by Christian sociologists. Christian ethical values can also influence how research is conducted and can, under some circumstances, facilitate communication between the researcher and those being studied (Poloma, 1980).

As important as these issues are, the focus of this book lies elsewhere. Here I am concerned primarily with the areas of philosophy called *epistemology* and *metaphysics*. Epistemology is the study of how we can reasonably claim to know things. An epistemological theory is a theory of how we attain worthwhile knowledge. On the other hand, metaphysics is the study of what exists. A metaphysician is a person who thinks in systematic and publicly accountable ways about the nature of reality—that is, about what exists, how it exists, and what valid statements can be made about it. Sociologists and Christians often make epistemological and metaphysical claims, even if they aren't aware of doing so.

Twenty years ago few sociologists thought of themselves as "metaphysicians." However, this self-image is changing of late due to the publication of several important books exploring the area known as the Sociology of Sociology. Within this subfield of study, the analytical tools of sociology have been turned on the discipline itself. What is revealed informs us about the metaphysical underpinnings of sociology. For reasons given in chapter 2, every science is based on certain untestable assumptions concerning the underlying nature of the world, of science itself, and (if it is a social science) of the nature of human nature and of social organization. In short, every sociological theory rests on metaphysical distinctions between what is "really real," what is only "apparently real," and what isn't real at all.

Since Christians share a world view that provides such distinctions, Christianity can be related to science—sociology in particular. In this respect, the warrant for producing a Christian sociology is as legitimate as that of humanistic and existential sociologies already commonly acknowledged.

Of course, the term *Christian sociology* does not mean that Christian sociologists have a more accurate and reliable way of encountering scientific truth. A Christian sociologist's study of racial prejudice, white-collar crime, or conformity within groups, will generally follow the same basic methodological procedures applicable to any other professional sociologist's work.

To repeat, Christian sociology claims no scientific methodology of its own, but it does claim a special metaphysic. To the degree that this metaphysic can shape sociological thinking, while still retaining the basics of the sociological perspective, is the degree to which *Christian sociology* is a useful term.

Christian sociology is a general orientation and not an explicit scientific theory. It is, as David Moberg writes, "an orientation within sociology by committed Christians who are sociologists" (1982, p. 3). Andrew Greeley (1977), a Catholic priest and sociologist, concurs. He claims that Christian sociology

> is not a set of principles from which one can derive with prior logic, practical policies and programs. It is rather a set of fundamental insights and assumptions about human nature and society that provide a perspective for looking at social reality (p. 130).

Christian sociologists typically make certain claims relevant to their work, such as the existence of a transcendent purpose to human history, the organismic nature of ideal society, and the nature and effects of human sinfulness. They also stress the limited scope of scientific inquiry, and the applicability of universal ethical standards whereby all social systems can be evaluated. While these assumptions are certainly not shared by all sociologists, some sort of assumptions about these issues are an inevitable part of all sociological theorizing at the abstract level. Moreover, such assumptions have a decided effect on the way in which sociologists "do sociology."

Fig. 1 **Ideas Central to the Sociological
Perspective and to Evangelical Christianity**

The Sociological Perspective	Evangelical Christianity
1. The social world is humanly constructed.	The world was created by God.
2. Society is greater than the sum of its parts.	Society is equal to the sum of its parts.

There are two major ideas central to the sociological perspective which sharply contrast with two corresponding ideas within evangelical Christianity, ideas expressed in figure 1. These two sets of ideas correspond to the book's two major parts. In Part 1, Christian dogma is used to critique and partially "rehabilitate" secular sociology. In particular, the issue of sociological relativity and its challenge to Christian absolutism is the dominant theme. In Part 2, the sociological perspective, developed in Part 1, will be used to critique evangelicalism and the cultural baggage it has picked up in its development as an American middle-class movement. Individualistic assumptions about the nature of society conducive to ideological conservatism and associated with contemporary evangelicalism will be examined and critiqued.

These two problems—relativity and ideology— are the two central issues. Of course, these are not the only issues confronting Christians who want to think sociologically, but I am convinced they are among the most pervasive and perplexing. Moreover, they often serve as rallying points for a host of more general metaphysical and epistemological issues that are raised whenever religion and science meet.

TYPES of Integration

There are a number of ways to approach the subject of integrating Christian faith and learning in any scientific discipline. Each approach has its own assumptions about the nature of Christian and disciplinary truth claims. Carter and Narramore (1979) identify four "ideal-type" approaches:

1. *Faith against learning.* This approach assumes that the logic and empirical methods of science are contrary to religious faith. Christians who take this approach assume that the Bible is the sole source of truth and that science can yield only a sophisticated form of error. Integration is therefore neither desired nor warranted. Most people who take this position usually apply it selectively to certain areas of knowledge—for example, to the question of origins.
2. *Faith in learning.* This approach begins with the assumption that there is considerable overlap between the truth claims of Christianity and science, but that science yields more reliable and valid information about the world than religion. Here we find an effort to integrate the two only insofar as they do not conflict. Where the Bible appears to make claims that are unscientific (such as miracles), biblical interpretation is adjusted ("demythologized") to fit with contemporary learning.
3. *Faith parallels learning.* Proponents of this view conclude that religion and science belong to wholly separate spheres of knowledge, and that one cannot be meaningfully translated into the terms of the other. This view claims that scientific knowledge is established on the basis of inductive logic, whereas religious faith is based on deductive logic. The two spheres of knowledge also appeal to different data sources (for instance, the "rational" study of nature vs. the "irrationality" of religious beliefs) and use entirely different research methods (experimentation vs. exegesis). Integration is therefore unthinkable.
4. *Faith integrates learning.* Proponents argue that there is one ultimate source of all truth, and that when properly understood, nature/science and revelation/Christianity cannot therefore be contradictory. Both the Bible and nature are complementary sources of truth. As a result, when they are considered separately, each one is, of necessity, incomplete as to the revelation of God's truth. The dichotomy between faith and learning claimed by advocates of the "faith parallels learning" position is denied here. Faith is as much a part of science as it is of religion; metaphysical claims underlie all efforts to know the truth.

Therefore, there is a reciprocal influence between religious faith and scientific discipline—each informing the other.

Objections to the idea of Christian sociology can be expected to arise on the basis of the particular approach the critic espouses. This book is written from a standpoint sympathetic to (but not in every respect synonymous with) position 4: "faith integrates learning." I anticipate, however, that many sociological critics will approach from the "faith parallels learning" position 3. I will argue that position 3 typically assumes too much about science because it doesn't adequately appreciate the importance of metaphysical assumptions underlying all scientific theory. Even so, I will argue that the integrative fit between the two perspectives is far from complete.

Other objections are expected. For example, some who support position 2 ("faith in learning") will point out that there is no single unified system of Christian metaphysics. Therefore, the phrase "Christian sociology" assumes too much; perhaps *a* Christian sociology can be produced, but certainly not *the* Christian sociology. I agree. However, it is unreasonable to conclude that any effort at producing Christian sociology is automatically invalid since metaphysical unity has not yet been achieved. After all, theoretical unity has not yet been achieved in sociology, yet one still speaks meaningfully of sociology as a single discipline (Ritzer, 1980).

The FOCUS of Integrative Efforts

What constitutes "integration" and what does it accomplish? While my answers to these questions may not be as definitive as we could wish, I do have a clear idea as to what integration is *not*. For example, integration is not accomplished by dusting a mixture of Christian terms and Scripture verses over ordinary science—what Blamires calls "secular thinking trimmed with pious platitudes" (1978, p. 41). Sociology does not become "Christian" merely because Scripture references are scattered throughout an otherwise secular text.[2]

---

2. Nor should we refer to essays on contemporary criticism written from a Christian ethical perspective as "integrative." There are a large number of books by Christian authors—some of them sociologists—on issues such as religious cults, nuclear war, marriage

Fig. 2 **Continuum of Efforts to Integrate Christian and Sociological Orientations**

concrete
specific
applications

general
metaphysical
assumptions

In general terms, efforts to integrate Christian and sociological orientations can be arranged on the continuum illustrated in figure 2. Many efforts to integrate Christianity with sociology belong at the left end of this continuum. For example, a Christian criminologist may discuss Roman justice with reference to appropriate biblical passages, such as the ones that describe Paul's trial in the courts of Felix, Festus, and Agrippa (Acts 24 and 25); or a lecturer analyzing racial ideologies could compare the assumptions of North American racism with ancient Roman and Greek ideologies relevant to biblical references to slavery. By so doing, sociologists can relate particular pieces of information from both areas.

At the other extreme, some authors seek to integrate the two domains of knowledge at the highest level of abstraction. Thus we are told that "all truth is God's truth," or that "Christ is our ultimate role model." As statements of religious faith, they are helpful in setting the moral tone of integrative efforts, but they contribute little to our efforts to understand how particular fields of knowledge, such as sociology, specifically relate to Christianity, and vice versa.

I believe that a more helpful form of integration falls between the extremes of particular scriptural applications and abstract assertions. Consequently, while specific applications and general orientations are included, the focus of this book falls in the area between these two.

Mutual Challenge

It is easier to say what integration of faith and learning is *not* than to say what it *is*. And it is easier to say what it *is* than to do

---

and family relations, and a host of contemporary personal problems, from loneliness to stress management. Many of these books do not constitute an integrative effort because, most importantly, they are not particularly sociological, which means they do not draw upon sociological theory to inform and orient their analyses. These books represent Christian commentary more than anything else.

it. Nevertheless, I will seek to at least juxtapose sociological and Christian ways of looking at the social world, and in so doing, will show how each perspective can challenge the other in mutually beneficial ways.

Christianity challenges sociologists to apply their analytical perspective to matters that count, to profit from biblical insights and values, and to be motivated by the desire to see God's kingdom established. On the other hand, sociology challenges Christians to escape our built-in parochial frame of reference, to be consistent in our application, to recognize that various cultural expressions of Christianity represent interpreted (and thus incomplete and biased) social perspectives, and to deal honestly and in an informed way with the consequences of this fact.

Whatever else it is, *social science is a metaphysical exercise.* As such, Christian metaphysics can inform us as to where we should begin our inquiry and where we ought to end up. Also, whatever else it is, *Christianity is a collective human endeavor.* As such, sociology can inform us how we typically go about being religious in a social way.

Part 1

Looking
at the Problem
of Relativity

Like all introductory efforts, we will begin at the beginning, that is, with an examination of the goals and methods of each participant in the dialogue. Christianity and sociology have very different purposes; one is a religion and the other tries to be a science, and in these differences we have the source of the tensions that exist.

The focus throughout the book is on the complex interrelationships between orthodox Christianity and sociology. There are two major ideas central to the sociological perspective which sharply contrast with two corresponding ideas within evangelical Christianity, ideas expressed in figure 1, page 20. (These correspond to the two sections of this book, as mentioned in the Introduction.)

In chapter 1, I discuss the scientific status of sociology. The scientific method represents a disciplined effort to promote accurate observation by means of certain methodological techniques.

The point of such observation is to test theories—the compilation of which represents the chief end of all sciences. The observational methods of science are designed to increase our confidence that what we observe is accurate, and what we conclude is valid. In doing so, scientists carefully restrict themselves to events which can be observed repeatedly by independent observers.

The first chapter sets forth both the promises and the limitations of the scientific approach as applied to social events. In so doing, the chapter highlights the subjectivity of human perception and builds a foundation for our appreciation of the skepticism of science, and of sociology in particular.

In chapter 2, I defend the thesis that values are a fundamental part of the scientific enterprise. Moreover, the argument is made that social scientific theories necessarily incorporate untestable values—assumptions about human nature and the social order. From this understanding, it can be asserted that orthodox Christians make some important assumptions relevant to sociological theory that others are less likely to make. It is on this basis that sociology and Christianity can speak to each other.

In chapter 3, the idea of subjectivity is explored further. Here, I outline the basic theme common to most contemporary sociological theories—that is, that social reality is a humanly constructed product. Among other factors, this claim means that definitions of social reality are relative to particular social contexts. Therefore, from an empirical perspective (which is the perspective of sociology), definitions of social reality vary according to their social contexts.

Chapter 3 also introduces the various methods of "debunking" as well as the main difficulty that Christian students usually experience in beginning sociology courses. As it is ordinarily taught, secular sociology appears to come down full force against the absolutist claims of Christianity—debunking these claims as "mere products of social contexts and interests," and thereby undermining the credibility of orthodox beliefs.

In chapter 4 several conceptual distinctions are introduced, the chief of which is between "cultural relativity" (which represents the factual foundation of the discipline), and "metaphysical relativism" (which is an untestable and therefore nonscientific claim that no absolute truths can be humanly known). The real and imagined corrosive effects of secular sociological thought are explored here, endeavoring to show how the relativistic approach of sociology is compatible with Christian absolutism.

Let's begin, then, with an effort to understand what it means to be scientific, and how sociologists approach the discipline in this manner.

1

The Nature of Science

Each science has its own unique subject matter. Physicists study the properties of matter. Biologists study life. Psychologists study the human psyche. But what do sociologists study? No doubt something to do with society.

Actually, most people do not have a clear idea of what sociologists do (besides teach sociology). In the first chapter of his book *Invitation to Sociology* (1963), Peter Berger discusses several popular yet inaccurate images of the sociologist. One of the most common misleading images is that of the sociologist as a person who "works with people." Many students assume that knowledge of sociology will enable them to help others in need. Therefore, they assume that sociologists are persons who are "professionally concerned with edifying activities on behalf of individuals and the community at large" (p. 2).

This image is partially correct, which means it is also partially incorrect. While it is true that many—perhaps all—of those recruited to professional sociology seek to improve the lot of humanity, it is nevertheless inaccurate to say that the advancement of humanitarian goals is the primary purpose of sociology.

Of course, there is no reason why a sociologist cannot be a humanitarian (and a Christian, for that matter). While sociologists and students studying sociology are often motivated by altruistic values, it is still true that these particular values and the general purpose of sociology (or any other science) are not identical: complementary, yes; synonymous, no.

Quite often, as Berger notes, students who have this image confuse sociologists with social workers. These students are usually surprised to learn that sociology and social-work courses are not even included within the same academic curriculum at most colleges. That's because social work is the practice of helping people—a practice which seeks to improve the lot of clients who need professional services. By contrast, sociology is not a practice at all, nor can it be if it seeks (as it does) to be a science. Sociology can provide a theoretical base for the practice of social work, but the purposes of the two disciplines are not the same.

Scientific Explanations: The Purpose of Sociology

Sociologists seek to understand the nature of social reality in a disciplined way. This fact tends to put sociologists on the defensive because many students think that their understanding of social reality is quite adequate without the assistance of sociology.

Why should anyone need a specialized science of society to help them understand what is already perfectly obvious? Even so, while most nonsociologists do not regard social reality as problematic, sociologists do. They are habitually dissatisfied with what is commonly known about it. For instance, commonly accepted knowledge can sometimes be shown to be incorrect. In fact, common knowledge about social reality is the very point about which sociologists suspend belief.

We sociologists, therefore, do not begin our study of society by assuming that what everyone believes to be true is true. Nor do we assume that it is necessarily false. Instead, sociologists suspend belief in what most people *know* to be true and search for better evidence.

But to recognize so-called better evidence when we see it, we need to establish acceptable standards by which we can judge which evidence *is* better. We can begin to understand how scientific evidence is evaluated (and thereby increase our understanding of the goals of sociology) by stating what is obvious: that to scientists, not all explanations are equally acceptable.

To be *acceptable,* explanations must conform to certain ground rules of scientific procedure. Three of these common rules concern *formality, measurement,* and *testability.* These are not the only rules, but by considering each, we will better understand sociology's purposes and methods as a science, which is the chief purpose of this chapter. Furthermore, certain topics will thereby be introduced which will serve us well in later chapters.

First, *acceptable scientific explanations must be formally stated.* For example, to be acceptable, scientific explanations (that is, theories) must be presented so that they do not violate certain canons of logic. It is illogical to account for event X in terms of event Z, if Z is a constant (that is, when measured, Z does not change). Something that does not change cannot possibly explain something that does change.[1]

Another logical requirement concerns the avoidance of circular explanations. If, for example, a theory explains why some people are racially prejudiced in terms that are largely synonymous with prejudice itself (like *intolerance*), then we haven't really accomplished much. If we explain that certain people are prejudiced because they are intolerant, then all we've done is beg the question.

Second, *adequate scientific explanations must refer to events that are measurable.* Even if the explanation is as general as "Event X is more likely to occur if event Y occurs first," the criterion of measurement is met. The phrases "more likely to occur" and "occurs first" are references—albeit quite vague—to measurements, and some degree of measurement must be involved in formulating scientific explanations.

The event to be explained is referred to as "the *dependent variable.*" It is dependent because it presumably does not occur unless another event ("the *independent variable*") occurs first. The word *variable* is used because the measurements of the event in question vary—that is, they are not constant.

---

1. This requirement is the reason why most references to "human nature" in scientific theories are not very helpful, if by this we mean a fixed "essence" of humanity.

Scientists begin their search for potential explanatory propositions (*hypotheses*) by comparing situations involving covariations among the events in question. Let's consider a simple illustration: suppose we want to know why it sometimes rains. Our existing theory tells us that rain (the dependent variable) is explained by the combination of falling temperature and rising humidity (the independent variables). In other words, it will rain, given a certain covariation between the amount of moisture in the air and falling temperatures. To test this theory, we would have to conduct laboratory conditions whereby we could artificially manipulate these independent variables, comparing them so as to determine the conditions whereby condensation is produced.

To give a different example, suppose we want to explain interracial prejudice. Our existing theory tells us that increased racial prejudice among members of a racial group against another racial group is explained (in part) by the event of increased economic competition between the groups. To test this hypothesis, we would probably have to compare typical interracial relations under different economic conditions.

Whether it is rain or prejudice we seek to explain, one or more variables is presumed to account for the variation in another event.

The point of this discussion about variables is that without the possibility of measurement, potential explanations cannot be tested. Consequently, they are not accepted as scientific explanations. Therefore, *the second rule of science concerns the measurement of events.*

Raising the issue of adequacy in scientific explanations and the necessity of measurement helps to introduce the third ground rule of science: *all scientific explanations must be testable.* In order for a theory to be acceptable, it must be stated in such a way that its validity can be tested and retested by independent observers.

Scientific Skepticism and Human Bias

Why all this concern with testability? Because underlying all scientific work is the assumption that humans are biased—that their perceptive abilities are limited and their perceptions are distorted. Yet, despite this skepticism, the goal of science remains to obtain information about how events are actually related to each other. We observe that planets move in conjunction with each other, that rain falls when the temperature changes, that interracial hostility increases when the economy falters. When we make such observations, we suspect that one event is caused by others. Whatever the relationships between the variables (causal or otherwise), scientists want a factual (*objective*) account, not someone's (*subjective*) opinion.

The word *objective* refers to the actual qualities of the object being studied, such as the events of planetary motion, precipitation, and intergroup conflict. On the other hand, the word *subjective* refers to the qualities of the observer, the subject who perceives the object.

The point is that scientists assume all humans are inescapably subjective creatures. Our perception of events is never purely objective, although most nonscientists (and even some scientists) talk and act as if it were. For example, people sometimes make statements like "This meat tastes bad," as if *badness* were an intrinsic quality of the meat. Rather, badness is a subjective evaluation. After all, what to us is a yukky bowl of grubs may be a perfectly acceptable (perhaps even *delicious*) meal for an Arunta tribesman. *Yukky* and *delicious, good* and *bad* are evaluations that tell us more about the subjectivity of the observer than about the objective properties of what is observed.

Science is a disciplined attempt to reduce human subjectivity. When we perceive objects, we do so in biased ways. One of the reasons for this bias (and the measurement variation that results) arises from the fact that we are creatures of culture. Our culture—that is, our system of shared meanings—conditions us to recognize only those events we have learned to recognize. We know about tape recorders because we have grown up in a culture in which tape recorders have a meaningful place. If I hurled a tape recorder at members of a technologically simple society, they would see the object coming, but they would not identify it as a tape recorder.

One of our family's leisure activities demonstrates this point rather well. We enjoy telling each other "minute mysteries." Try solving this one:

A man and his young son are seriously injured in an automobile accident. They are brought by ambulance to a local hospital where they are put into adjoining emergency-surgery rooms. The chief surgeon enters the room where the boy is being prepared for the operation and declares, "I cannot operate on this boy. He is my son."

What's going on here?

Unless you have heard this mystery before, you may have a hard time coming up with a feasible explanation. (In fact, when I use this particular mystery in class to illustrate cultural bias, less than 5 percent of my students solve it within two minutes.) The solution does not involve foster fathers, miraculous recoveries, mistaken identities, or other such possibilities. The solution is simple; the surgeon is the boy's mother.

Pretty obvious, right? It may be obvious now, but if you were part of the 95 percent who apparently do not think of surgeons as women, then you will have to admit that the solution was not so obvious. Because we live in a sexist society, we have learned to "see" reality in a sexist way, that is, we expect surgeons to be men. In this sense, so-called reality conforms to what we have experienced. (Soviet students would have less difficulty with our mystery because a much higher percentage of Soviet surgeons are women.)

The conclusions of many cross-cultural studies of perception support this point. In one such study, James Bagby, a social psychologist, simultaneously projected slides onto a screen, superimposing the images. One set of slides was of a baseball game and a bullfight. When shown simultaneously, the audience in the bleachers merged into one scene, but the player at bat and the bullfighter were distinct. The slides were shown to separate groups of Mexican and American children. The images were left on the screen for only a fraction of a second, enough for most of the Mexican children to report seeing a bullfight, and for most of the American children to report seeing a baseball game (Bagby, 1957). In effect, there is more to seeing than meets the eye.

No one doubts that the image of the bullfight showed up on the retinas of the American children. North Americans, however, learn to filter out "nonsense" like bullfights and recognize only the image of the ball game. Such are the wonders of human perception.

Our perceptions of reality are fundamentally subjective. Most people readily acknowledge this point. Scientists differ from most people, however, in the unrelenting consistency with which they apply this insight to their understanding of the world.

Human perception, then, is always distorted (biased) and hence subjective. In effect, there is a cultural lens ever before our eyes (and our other senses)—a filter through which, in ordinary circumstances, only preselected, culturally designated meanings can pass.

As humans subject to the frailties of the human condition, we cannot rightfully claim perfect (that is, objective) observation and thereby claim perfect knowledge. If we do, we make ourselves gods. From a Christian perspective, such a notion is heretical.

On the matter of human powers of observation and knowledge, there is a striking compatability between the Christian and the scientific ways of looking at things. Underlying both perspectives is the assumption that humans are imperfect beings and that our perception and understanding are inherently flawed. Both the Christian and the scientist want perfect sight, objective information; but such is not possible, and we know it (or at least we ought to know it).

As Christians and as social scientists, our response ought not be frustration and resignation. Christians are instructed to seek perfection, but also to be patient, to work diligently because the kingdom is at hand, to trust God, and to ask for divine guidance. In the meantime, we continually struggle with our fallen nature, and work toward that day when perfection will be possible.

What, then, of the sociologist? Remember that the third rule for acceptable scientific explanation concerns *testability;* we must be able to observe repeatedly and measure the relationships between the dependent and independent variables. Moreover, these measurements must be available to independent observers. If all humans are biased, then the best scientists can do is to carry on their research in a manner designed to reduce bias to a minimum.

The basic principle behind scientific efforts to minimize bias is rather straightforward: the more observers who observe the same happening, in the same setting, under the same conditions, and the more their observations conform to the same conclusion, the more objective (that is, *accurate*) and the less subjective (that is, *imaginary*) the perceptions are assumed to be.

This is a common insight. Notice how we usually check out our perceptions with other people, particularly if what we think we've observed is at all unusual:

"Did you see that?"

"Is it cold in here, or is it just me?"

"Did you think that last exam was fair?"

The methodological device of multiple independent observations is related to one other assumption about human perception: observers are not necessarily equally biased. Although we assume all scientific knowledge is incomplete and must be held tentatively (because all humans are biased), we also assume that careful training in methodological procedure and commitment to the goal of scientific integrity will increase observational accuracy. Furthermore, as scientists learn about how perceptual biases operate, they can often reduce the effects of bias in subsequent studies. For example, studies like Bagby's demonstrate that perceptual bias can be measured. Such studies tell us how cultural bias operates and give us useful clues as to how we might minimize its effects. Therefore, professional training and the accumulation of scientific findings on bias are essential to the progress of scientific knowledge.

Suppose, for example, we wanted to know the relationship between religiosity (that is, the orthodoxy of church members) and their attitudes toward other races (that is, their degree of racial prejudice). If we conducted a study, we might observe that the more orthodox white people are, the more likely they are to be racially prejudiced against blacks. In fact, many researchers have observed precisely this relationship (Wuthnow, 1973).

What if, however, we hired only irreligious white researchers to conduct such a study? Might we expect them to be influenced by the fact that they are white and irreligious? Of course. Then again, we could expect other biases from blacks and/or highly religious people. Since we expect that everyone is biased in some fashion, what we need in order to test adequately the thesis are independent studies, conducted by properly trained observers who reflect various biases. Then, if these studies yield similar results, we would be justified in concluding that we are at least approaching what is objectively true on the matter.[2]

Intersubjective Verifiability

At the heart of every science is the requirement to produce data associated with conclusions that could be potentially refuted by others. The scientific method is actually a complicated way of determining who's telling the truth and who isn't. Repeatable events are therefore the cornerstone of all scientific activity. The assumption that reproducible results reduce the effects of human bias is the epistemological foundation of all claims for scientific objectivity.

However, to call this knowledge "objective" is to miss the point. Knowledge is only as valid as the means whereby it is attained, and the methods scientists use to obtain knowledge cannot eliminate human subjectivity. Therefore, we need to refer to the methods of science not as *objective* but as *intersubjective,* and the methodological process of science as *intersubjective verifiability.* Granted, it's not a phrase that falls trippingly from the tongue, but as a description of scientific knowledge, it is a whole lot more honest than the word *objective.*

The phrase *intersubjective verifiability* means that science proceeds on the basis of multiple independent observations by persons who we assume are biased (that is, whose perceptions are subjective) but who are trained to be aware of bias and who take disciplined methodological steps to reduce these effects to a feasible minimum.

---

2. Of course, the truth of a scientific claim is relative to the proposition in question. Perhaps it is true that religious people are more prejudiced. Even so, it is unlikely that this is all that can be said on the matter. Could it also be true (even truer?) that certain kinds of religious people are less prejudiced than other kinds?

Theories can always be reformulated in this way and more tests conducted. Since we'll never see the end to this process, it is unwise to ever speak of scientific truths as being final or proven.

For these reasons, then, the word *objectivity* ought not to be used—except to indicate the unreachable goal of science: that is, the elusive quest for undistorted perception and nonbiased knowledge. Similarly, if the word *proof* suggests a final truth, it ought to be eliminated from scientific discourse.[3] How can anything ever be scientifically proven when evidence is forever incomplete?

For scientific observations to be intersubjectively verifiable, the events studied must be capable of being measured by multiple scientists, working independently. Events capable of repeated measurements by independent observers are called *empirical events*. By definition then, science is limited to empirical events.

The distinction between empirical and nonempirical events is basic to any discussion of science. Furthermore, the successful integration of science and Christianity is impossible unless this distinction is kept firmly and clearly in mind. All sorts of problems arise if we do not try to distinguish between empirical and nonempirical matters.

Muslims say there is one God. Christians say there are three Gods, but that they operate as one. Animists say there aren't any gods at all (but each object has a "spirit"), whereas Hindus say there are thousands of them. To the sociologist (thinking as sociologists think), all these claims are, well, just that—claims. This is the case whether the sociologist in question happens also to be a committed Hindu, Muslim, Christian, or (for all I know) animist. Whatever their religious beliefs, they will all have to set the question of the actual number of gods aside while doing sociology and thinking sociologically. This ascetic response is not a matter of personal style; it is a response dictated by the nature of gods and the limited scope of science. There simply is

---

3. Of course, the word *proof* should not be eliminated entirely. In those disciplines that rely on *deductive* logic (that is, those that start with a general premise and logically deduce more specific conclusions: disciplines like theology and mathematics), the word *proof* is appropriate and useful. However, science starts with particular sensate observations (i.e., the biased kind) and uses them *inductively* to build a general conclusion.

The two most notable methods of arriving at truth by means of these two forms of logic—the scientific (inductive) and the metaphysical (deductive)—have obvious relevance to our efforts to relate sociology and Christianity. They will therefore be examined in greater detail later.

no adequate empirical test to determine the correct number of gods. This is purely a metaphysical question.

Therefore, we have two types of truth claims here: the fact that truth claims vary (that is, a question of *morés*—different groups claim different truths) and the ultimate truth of those various metaphysical claims (a question of *morals*—whose moral claims are actually true?). Only the former is an empirically testable matter. While the two types of truth claims (morés and morals) do tend to merge, it is helpful to conceptually distinguish between them. Students of sociology who are unable to distinguish between morés and morals will run into all sorts of problems.

Empirical vs. Normative: The Case of Conversion

The boundaries of science are drawn by the application of empirical methods. A nonempirical event cannot be explained using the methods of science. Consider religious conversion, for example. Evangelical Christians identify themselves on the basis of their relationship with Jesus Christ, initiated by means of personal conversion. But which persons have been truly converted? Can anyone know for sure? Certainly not the social scientist because this question does not refer to an empirical event.[4]

Even so, there are aspects of the conversion process that *are* open to intersubjective verification. For example, a behavioral scientist interested in this phenomenon could study a sample of persons claiming to have experienced conversion. Although we cannot tell whether a conversion is real or not by means of empirical test, we can intersubjectively observe the relationships between the claim of conversion and certain other variables that may also be involved.

---

4. Nor can Christians who take the Bible seriously know with certainty, because in it we read that among those who claim to be Christians are many imposters (*see* Matt. 7:21–23).

Therefore, we are not in a position to judge another's Christian commitment since good deeds are not significant in themselves (1 Cor. 13:3). As sociologists, we may be able to intersubjectively measure *good deeds* (that is, deeds defined by a particular group as "good"), but we cannot intersubjectively measure so-called true Christian commitment. In fact, we are warned by Christ not even to try to make that judgment (Matt. 7:1-5).

Which subgroups of our population are most likely to be converted? What happens to people when they claim they have been converted? These questions and others like them involve empirical matters. Just as we can intersubjectively measure the temperature of a room or the height of every student in a class, so we can measure at least some of the effects of religious conversion. But again, we cannot empirically determine the truth of the claims of conversion, nor of any value—of which "conversion" is but one expression. The goal of scientifically determining the truth of a conversion will always be elusive because the claim of true conversion represents a moral assertion—a question of the truth of a value.

A value is a desired end-state, a personal preference for one state of affairs over another. Values therefore imply a moral or ethical choice based on personal beliefs. It is these beliefs that make value claims fall outside the boundaries of science. The reasons for this limitation are straightforward.

First, *the validity of the beliefs on which the values rest is not open to common measurement.* We can measure the level of prejudice (a matter of morés), but we cannot measure whether people ought to be less prejudiced (a matter of morals). A liberal will claim that racial prejudice is bad; a bigot will claim the opposite. Prejudice is based upon one's beliefs about the group in question. In other words, the truth claims of the values implied in prejudice are based on whether or not one believes certain factors to be true. Since this sort of belief reflects personal choices, scientists try to stay clear of the question by ruling the question of their truth out of bounds.

To repeat, we can scientifically study morés (that is, what people say ought to be true), but not morals (what is, in fact, true in a normative sense). It is one consideration for a sociologist to claim that "this group of feminists thinks men are inferior"; it is quite another to claim sociologists have demonstrated that men are inferior. It is possible for social scientists to study which groups are most likely to pray, but it is not possible for them to determine whether or not God hears prayers.

Second (and following from this idea of empirical limits of science), *intersubjective verifiability requires a common scale of measurement.* Before such measurements can be made, the independent and dependent variables in question need to be commonly defined. While complete agreement is not required, something other than total disagreement is necessary. Once preliminary definitional agreement exists (for example, for terms such as *religiosity* and *prejudice*), the events can be observed and measured with the use of a common measuring scale. To be satisfactory, it would have to be a scale that ideally gives the same quantified results to separate observers.[5]

Here's the point: scientists cannot get at the truth of any value because no common measurement scale could ever be devised to do so. The beliefs on which the values rest are too dependent on personal experience to allow for sufficient agreement. So what is "true conversion" to this Christian might be "false conversion" to another.[6] For the social scientist studying conversions (and speaking as a scientist), that's where the matter stands—regardless of the sociologist's religious beliefs.

Why Sociology Can Only Indirectly Help People

Having discussed the purpose and the limits of science, we now return to our original question, *Why can't sociology be used to help people?*

The answer should now be apparent: sociology cannot be defined in this way because the phrase *help people* suggests a value. One group may define a particular action as helpful, while another may define the same act as a pain in the neck.

Several college students got to know an elderly man who lived nearby. When the man went into the hospital for an operation, the students decided to help him by cleaning his home. When they arrived, the place was a wreck. His dog lived inside

---

5. Absolute precision is obviously not a reasonable criterion of scientific status. Scientists want only to be assured that the events in question can be intersubjectively measured with a common scale. Even so, the status of a science is often evaluated indirectly on the precision of its measurements. This makes physics "more scientific" than, say, biology, and sociology less scientific than either. All are sciences, however, since all produce testable theories.

6. Of course, most Christians think that they can identify reasonably well those who are not Christ's followers by watching their behavior, but good deeds alone will not tell us who is and who is not truly a Christian (Eph. 5; *see also* 2 Cor. 13:5, where Paul indicates Christians should continually scrutinize their own behavior: "Examine yourselves to see whether you are in the faith; test yourselves. Do you not realize that Jesus Christ is in you—unless, of course, you fail the test?")

without being let out regularly, the roof leaked, and nothing was ever put away. When the students left, the place was neat, clean, and it smelled a whole lot better.

At least it looked and smelled better from the students' point of view. However, this was not the perspective with which the old man viewed his world. When he returned home from the hospital, he took one look at his newly rearranged (and middle-classified) home, and called the cops. He charged the students with unlawful trespass into a residence—an offense punishable by two years in prison! The judge dismissed the charges with a warning, but not before the students had learned an important lesson about the variability of values.

The goal of professional social work is to help people, whereas the goal of sociology is to intersubjectively explain human interaction.[7] Even if we grant that these two disciplines have different purposes, is it not possible for sociology to inform the practice of social work? Of course, but note that scientific theories can be used for any purpose. An engineer who values American industrial productivity can use the theories of physics to build bridges connecting one part of our economic system with another, and thereby increasing its efficiency. Another engineer, working for the hoped-for revolutionary takeover, can use the theories of physics to blow up the same bridges.

Which is the so-called best use of physics? For reasons that should now be clear, this question is not one that any scientist can answer. Scientists can tell us how to build or blow up bridges; they can tell us what will probably happen if we do

---

7. There are some commonalities between the two disciplines, however. For one thing, social work has been getting more scientific of late, if by this term we mean the incorporation of careful procedures into their research. Even so, I have not identified science with respect to careful research, or even with intersubjective research; rather, science represents the use of such methods for the purpose of constructing testable empirical theory. Therefore, whatever the care of its procedures, as long as the primary purpose of social work is to help people, social work cannot be considered a science. A profession, yes; a science, no.

Besides, sociology is not the discipline most likely to supply scientific information to the social worker. For various complex social and political reasons, the typical social worker is usually more interested in adapting the presumably needy client to the presumably healthy social system, rather than in changing the system so as to meet the needs of its otherwise normal victims. What is perceived as needed (and social workers are generally encouraged to think this way) is knowledge about "maladapted *individuals*," not "malfunctioning *social systems*," which often turns social workers toward psychological theories and remedies and away from those of sociology.

either, for these are empirical matters and common measurement scales are available—but scientists cannot tell us whether or not we *ought* to build rather than blow up bridges. In the same respect, sociologists cannot tell us—as scientists—what we ought to do with our social scientific knowledge. Our science is insufficient in this respect and must be directed and applied by means of a moral perspective.[8]

Summary

We have distinguished between the purposes of sociology and other disciplines (like social work), which seek to apply a set of values. I have outlined the subjective nature of human perception, the intersubjective procedures of science, and the promises and limitations of science with respect to facts and values. In so doing, I hope the purpose and rationale for sociology as a scientific discipline is now clearer.

Although we have ranged rather far afield during this academic discussion of the scientific status of sociology, there has been a purpose behind it all. The ground covered thus far will be important in later discussions of the relationship between Christianity and sociology. However, the discussion of facts and values in the latter part of this chapter could leave the impression that science and human values are antithetical; that the scientific goal of objective knowledge could be reached if it were not for the subjectivity of values; that scientists are to do all they can to devalue their work; that their science fails to the degree that values influence their understanding of empirical events.

In other words, is it accurate to call sociology a value-free discipline? Since the response to this question will influence to a significant degree what we can subsequently claim for a Christian-sociology dialogue, we will turn our attention in the next chapter to the relationship between theological values and scientific facts.

---

8. This raises an important issue related to the subject of the next chapter: is there a qualitative difference between the types of beliefs shared by members of religious groups and the types of beliefs shared by members of scientific groups? I will argue that there is not—that the difference exists only because secular scientists wish to believe a qualitative difference exists.

2

Values and Science

Sociology's claim to scientific status rests on the intersubjectivity of its observations.

In the last chapter we saw how scientists must limit their studies to empirical events. In accepting this limitation, scientists claim their findings can be trusted since they are based on something more reliable than opinion. For this reason, and because the truth of a value cannot be established scientifically, scientists carefully distinguish between the realm of *objective facts* and the realm of *subjective values*. In this way people often speak of science as being *value free*.

The question of value freedom has been hotly contested in sociological circles ever since Max Weber coined the phrase in the early part of this century. Actually, a good deal of ink and body heat have been wasted in this effort, since the parties to the debate have frequently failed to acknowledge areas of wide consensus among scientists—even failing to carefully define terms like *objectivity,* so that all the participants in the debate use it to mean similar things. Therefore, I will start this discussion of facts and values by underscoring some common agreements among the debaters.

All scientists agree that the purpose of science is to explain empirical events. As such, scientists commit themselves to a

basic methodology involving systematic, disciplined observations of comparative situations (although scientists in each discipline have to work out their own methodological variations
suitable to the peculiar events they study). Underlying this commitment to the comparative method is the promise to tell the
truth as best they are able. This general agreement extends to a
set of related assumptions. *It is agreed that no one can advance
the cause of science, properly understood, by inventing stories
about what they observed.* Likewise, as we saw in chapter 1, *we
assume that human perception is subjective, and hence biased.* In
other words, all human observations are interpretations, and
are—for this reason alone—inevitably distorted. Of course, the
promise to tell the truth combined with the realization that all
perception is biased produces its own dilemma. Even so, whatever else is involved, all scientists promise to tell the truth as
best they are able. All agree that willful distortion is morally
unacceptable, that *other types of distortion are undesirable, and
that they can and should be reduced by applying the intersubjective methods of science (even though all agree that interpretation
and distortion cannot be eliminated).* In short, bias is not seen as
merely a temporary human shortcoming. It is inconceivable
that human perceptions could ever be anything other than subjective, but it *is* conceivable that the distortion can be reduced
further than what we have already achieved.[1] Finally, due to the
nature of scientific methodology, *all agree that the analytical
scope of science must be limited to empirical phenomena.* Scientists must not seek to determine the truth of values, for such
cannot be done.

These, then, are the widely shared agreements concerning
the purpose and orientation of science:

The purpose of science is to construct theories which explain;

---

1. There is an additional issue that should at least be noted here—that all efforts to
reduce bias take place within general models (or scientific paradigms). These models
represent ways of making sense of the world. As a model becomes dominant within a
scientific discipline, "normal science" can proceed by trying to eliminate bias intersubjectively. However, should a competing paradigm take its place (which is inevitable), the
attempt to achieve objectivity begins on new terms (compare with Thomas Kuhn, *The
Structure of Scientific Revolutions*).

Scientists must be committed to the comparative method and are committed to telling the truth about what they observe;

All forms of bias are undesirable and ought to be reduced as much as possible;

Scientists ought to restrict themselves to empirical events and for that reason they cannot comment on the truthfulness of any value claim.

Once this consensus is acknowledged, a clearer view of the relationship between science and values is achieved. The debate will not be resolved in this way but it will be more productive.

Science as a Value-based Process

Science, strictly speaking, is not value free. Values enter into all scientific work in a number of ways. For instance, each of the agreements about so-called proper science listed above are value statements. No one could empirically determine the truth of any of the values implied in the consensual position just discussed. In addition, all scientific work involves a number of different value-laden processes. Let's briefly examine four of these processes.

First, there is the process of *discovery*. What will be studied? Consider, for example, cancer research. A large percentage of our population will contract some form of cancer—a higher percentage today than was the case twenty years ago. It is therefore easy to understand why the search for its cause is receiving a good deal of expensive scientific research. But what will be investigated, and how will we go about investigating it? Consider these two alternative approaches: we could instruct our scientists to find the cures of cancers already contracted, or we could have them discover the sources of cancer. In short, we could concentrate on either curing or preventing cancer.

While we would certainly like to get valid answers for both questions, they are not now given equal scientific attention. On the one hand, there is not enough money to research both questions adequately. On the other, any effort to prevent cancer would soon come up against quite powerful groups who have strong interests in seeing to it that certain cancer-causing fea-

tures of our system stay intact. Consider environmental pollution, for example. Breathing the air around some industrial
plants is definitely unhealthy, but the cost of adequately cleaning up the air is more than most are willing to bear. Furthermore, what does it mean to "clean up the air adequately"? We
aren't likely to reach ready agreement here. For these reasons
and others, cancer researchers focus more on curing cancer than
in preventing it.

This may not be good medicine or ethics, but it *is* good politics.
The scientific work that goes on in the American Cancer In-
stitute is presumably the most thorough and precise scientific
work that money can buy. But all the empirical precision in the
world cannot transform the decision to cure rather than to prevent cancer into value-free science.

Deciding what will be studied, then, is a value-based process.
So too is the related process of *hypothesis formulation.* Proposing
a hypothesis for test (once it has been determined what will be
studied) is also influenced by value commitments. Theoretical
concepts are laced with value connotations. Words like *life,
nature, origins,* and *time*—indispensable concepts in many scientific theories—cannot be defined without implying certain
values and untestable beliefs. These commitments are even
more obvious in social scientific theories. Concepts like "balanced trade," "psychological abnormality," or "social deviance"
are impossible to define without implying a whole set of values
in each case.

To cite one concrete illustration, imagine that two research
teams are hired by the U.S. Department of Defense to study how
enlisted personnel adjust to military life. In the process of con-
ducting their research, both teams have to consider the phenomena of AWOL (absence without leave, a military offense). How
will they study it? What assumptions will they make?

Let us presume that one team is comprised of politically conservative psychologists. Without giving it much thought (if
any), the researchers might assume that AWOLs are "a problem." They would then proceed to study a carefully selected
sample of AWOLs, perhaps administer a battery of psychological tests, the results of which may indeed show that AWOLs are
generally unstable personalities.

The other team, comprised of politically radical sociologists, would probably start their study with an entirely different set of assumptions. (Granted, it takes quite an effort to imagine the army hiring such a research team, but try anyway.) Instead of assuming the AWOLs are "the problem," this team could assume that the army is the problem, since they define the military as a capitalist tool established for the purposes of controlling and exploiting the workers. In other words, to the radical sociologists, AWOLs are just normal people trying to bear up under unacceptable conditions. And behold, the sociologists' data support this hypothesis: lower class soldiers *are*, in fact, overrepresented in the lower ranks and underrepresented in the upper ranks. Not surprisingly, AWOLs are almost exclusively low-ranking soldiers. And so on.

The point here is simple: both research efforts may be as objective and empirical as they can possibly be, yet both reflect the subjective values of the scientists' divergent interpretations of reality. This is the case with every scientific research effort, although the influence might not always be so obvious. Even so, somebody's subjectivity will be interjected, even though the best objective methods are used.

So far, we have investigated the role of values in science in two of the major processes of scientific work: in the discovery process and in the formulation of hypotheses. A third process concerns *data interpretation*. Data do not interpret themselves. In fact, the word *data* (from the Latin word *datum:* "to be given") is misleading. Conclusions and even observations are *taken,* not given. The facts never present themselves objectively. Every so-called fact is an interpretation (including this one).

We all know people who, if they want to go someplace, will say, "Oh, it's just down the street," whereas an undesirable destination is "too far away," even though the distances may be similar. In the same manner, one sociologist may interpret "fully 65 percent" of a sample to have responded in a particular way, whereas another may say that "only 65 percent" gave that response. Similarly, evaluative criteria must be imposed which define certain statistical data as "significant," while other data is not.

A fourth way in which values are involved in science concerns the issue of *application*. How will scientific information be used?

Any use will have social consequences. It is therefore impossible to take a value-neutral position vis-à-vis scientific research. Researchers who insist that they are "just doing science" and on this basis, wish to remain free of values, cannot have their wish. *To do nothing is to do something.* The scientist who helps the government develop a new weapons system cannot legitimately claim that only the interests of neutral science are being served. This may seem pretty obvious, and yet I know scientists who sincerely claim such.

Those who argue for value-free science often state that science is only a tool; it can be used for any purpose. It is therefore neutral. The observation that science is a tool is valid—except that it ironically undermines the argument for value-free science. Those who pay millions of dollars for scientific information will see to it that the "tool" is used to advance both their interests and their values—which often conflict with the values of other groups.

There are other ways in which values are incorporated into scientific work, but I'll not enumerate them all here. Rather, let's direct our attention to what I regard as the most important issue concerning the question of value-free sociology—that is, the claim that all scientific theories must rest on a set of untestable value-based assumptions. It is this issue that provides us the opportunity to understand how Christianity can link up with science in general, and with sociology in particular.

The Metaphysical Basis of Sociological Theory

Every scientific theory is based on certain untestable assumptions. In sociology, these assumptions involve values concerning such issues as the nature of human nature (are people basically self-seeking creatures or not?), models of social order (is normative agreement more important in establishing social order than differential power?), and values regarding the purpose of the discipline (should sociologists seek merely to analyze social change, or should they seek to bring it about?).

These and other value-based assumptions are inescapable. All sociological theories start with assumptions on these and other issues; the position one takes cannot be based on empirical observations alone.

For example, sociologists know that normative agreement and unequal power are both involved in creating and maintaining social order, but which is the more "fundamental" or "primary" factor? The answer to this question reveals one's normative evaluation of our world (that is, one's values) and not simply what one has been able to intersubjectively observe and measure about society.

What is true for so-called mainstream sociology is certainly true for any of the more deliberately value-committed sociologies.

Logically enough, the presuppositions of Christian sociology are derived from interpretations of biblical revelation. I will briefly mention some of these presuppositions here, and then discuss each at greater length in the chapters to follow.

First, faced with a choice, *Christian sociologists tend to prefer philosophical idealism over materialism.*[2] Idealists claim that the ultimate reality (or driving force) of history is ideas, not material forces. While Christian social scientists recognize the causal importance of material forces (such as the predominant type of technological production), they will not regard these forces as the sole or even the primary cause.

In the beginning was not the *deed*—the means of production, the unequal distribution of political control, or a class system. The Christian asserts that in the beginning was the *Word*—the mind of God, and the human minds created in the divine image.[3]

Christians cannot agree with those who attribute little or no analytical significance to the human mind and to its capacity to create symbols—symbols which in turn direct human activity. Christian sociologists will seek to keep the creative capacity of

---

2. Obviously, I do not speak for all Christian sociologists. Nor am I implying that most sociologists (or even any of them) take an extreme idealist or materialist position—only that, insofar as one position is preferred over the other (which is usually the case), idealism will be preferred.

3. Again, my purpose is not to suggest that one must choose either materialism or idealism. We can believe in both the means of production *and* the mind of God. But insofar as one force tends to shoulder the other aside as the ultimate cause of history (as I believe is usually the case), Christians ought to stay with the mind of God.

As we will see in the next chapter, I have not abandoned materialistic forces and their effect on human thought. It is not necessary to choose ideas over material conditions. I am content with one famous materialist's summation of the relationship between materialistic determinism and idealistic self-determinism: "Men make history, but they do not make it exactly as they please."

the human mind in the forefront of their theoretical imagery (Burwell, 1981a; Lyon, 1982). Correspondingly, Christian sociology will not be content to view humans as mechanisms entirely determined by impersonal social forces, even though it can be empirically demonstrated that these forces do strongly influence our thought and behavior. Although scientific determinism may be acknowledged more in certain areas of theoretical analysis than in others, a thoroughgoing determinism is not deemed acceptable.

Christian sociologists will not agree that the human mind is merely a reflection of economic, political, or social interests. Taken to the extreme, such a view implies that I must define sociology the way I do here solely because I am a white, middle-class, Christian, American male. To adopt this position would be tantamount to doing away with sociology itself, since there wouldn't be any point to it under such conditions. After all, a thoroughly deterministic sociology does not allow for the possibility of controlling bias to any degree. What, then, is the point of science? More importantly, a thoroughgoing determinism contradicts the Christian view of human nature, which incorporates aspects of freedom and responsibility (MacKay, 1974).

Christian sociologists are among those who recognize that sociology and ethics are inseparable. While acknowledging that humans create a collective sense of reality, including ethical reality, Christian sociologists refuse to assume that all ethics are mere human creations, and hence relative. Such a position assumes that there are no absolute truths, since it is also assumed that all claims as to what is real (hence, true) must be evaluated solely in terms of the social context in which the claims are made. Such relativism is contrary to orthodox Christian thought.

Christian sociologists begin with a different set of assumptions. It will not do to sort out the nonempirical parts (as if that could be done) and turn them over to religion, and to sort out the empirical parts and turn these over to sociology—each in its own neatly appropriate sphere. This is a false dichotomy. Believing and looking are not separate activities. The distinction is useful, to be sure, but claiming a dichotomous distinction is naive.

Insofar as they contest for the same truth, I do not think that sociological understanding dominates Christian understanding, although this is the way it seems to work for most sociologists I know. By contrast, I accord greater validity to biblical images of human nature and social order than I do the so-called findings of social and behavioral scientists on these subjects. Even so, as I will try to show later, I do not perceive these two ways of looking at and understanding the world as necessarily contradictory. We should be about the business of finding out what truths may be consistently understood by means of all available approaches.

There is yet another aspect to the question of value relativity and sociological knowledge: any neatly drawn dichotomy between religion and sociology will inevitably contribute to the view that there is no objective basis to values—that all values reflect mere subjective states, relative to particular times and circumstances. That may well be a modern idea, but it is not an orthodox Christian idea.

Not only that, but such relativism undermines the moral order which sustains social interaction. The growth of this sort of relativism—so widespread in the West today—is a main reason why an integration of Christian and sociological thought is needed now. The kind of sociology that eschews absolute values (so-called naturalistic sociology) has as one of its major unintended consequences the erosion of any and all forms of public morality on which social order is based.

To make this claim is not to say that naturalistic sociology is distinctly immoral—only that relativism undermines all moral systems.[4] When sociology transforms the perception of its students into seeing social reality as nothing more than a tempo-

---

4. Of course, morality can be imposed in exploitative ways. Nevertheless, even those who rest their entire theoretical position on conflict and power differentials must also recognize that these forces are inadequate to establish in themselves a durable and coordinated system of interaction. Even some Marxian sociologists are beginning to recognize the need for a morally based order in society. (See Richard Quinney's *Providence: The Reconstruction of Social and Moral Order.* New York: Longman, 1980.)

My remarks should not be interpreted to mean that any particular social order has the stamp of Christian morality upon it.

rary adjustment to an arbitrary set of social conditions, it represents a distinct threat to more than just Christians. Many of the disturbing features of modern society can be tied to this growing sense of ethical relativism. After all, why should we care about the welfare of others if the obligation to do so is perceived as arbitrarily drawn (or worse yet, imposed on us by our oppressors)? The degree to which a society ceases to encourage moral obligation is the degree to which that social order is on its way either to collapse or (more likely) to some form of tyranny (Bendix, 1971).

These remarks are established on yet other assumptions, for example, that typical members of any society tend to first seek their own individual or group's welfare unless there is an internalized moral imperative to do otherwise. This attribute of conservative thought (that humans are, by nature, selfish) is consistent with the orthodox view of innate sin and is generally accepted by Christian sociologists as normative.

A more complete Christian image of human nature, however, incorporates the divine command to resist this selfish tendency. Christ told his followers to treat others as they would have others treat them (Matt. 22:39), and Paul exhorted Christians to consider the interests of others as important as they do their own in making decisions (Phil. 2:3, 4).

In sum, Christian sociologists tend to stress the causal importance of ideas over material realities in their views of human action, rejecting the extreme positions of materialism, determinism, and ethical relativism. They selectively incorporate certain aspects of both classical conservative and radical thought, as difficult as these may be to hold in combination.

Note that none of these issues can be resolved on a strictly empirical basis. The claim of a distinctly "Christian sociology"—incorporating as it does a metaphysical foundation to its empirical superstructure—does not represent a unique feature: *all* sociological schools incorporate metaphysical claims into their theories. Christian sociology represents one self-conscious attempt to declare that values *do* undergird all scientific theorizing, and that these values have significant effects on sociological thought. Stating the relationship between science and values this way is motivated by the understanding that if we don't base our work on Christian assumptions, then someone else's assumptions will have to be used.

Value-free Sociology?

If by *value-free sociology* we mean that sociologists must strive to be as objective as possible, that we ought to distinguish as best we can between statements of fact and statements of value, and that we should recognize that the truth claims of values cannot be validated by scientific procedure, then I am a supporter of value-free sociology. There is a substantial difference between explanation and evaluation, analysis and advocacy, and, like most sociologists, I attempt to differentiate between the two. If, however, we mean to imply that science operates free of any and all value presuppositions—that "Christian," "feminist," "humanistic," or any other value-based sociology is simply a contradiction in terms—then I do not support the notion.

The process of scientific inquiry, hypothesis formation, interpretation, and application are intrinsically value-based. Of course, this conclusion does not mean that science is identical to metaphysics, any more than it means intersubjectivity is identical to subjectivity. The disciplined procedures of science are able to control bias significantly, and they ought to be valued and protected on this basis. However, even the most careful and methodologically refined scientific procedures represent some application of values, theological or otherwise. Science stands on philosophical shoulders.

I reemphasize this point for the benefit of those who argue that there is a sharp line between objective science and subjective values, between sociology and theology—rejecting on this basis the claims of Christian sociology.[5] A general distinction between fact and value needs to be made, but we ought not draw too fine a line in doing so.

Such ambiguity need not be seen as evidence of failure. Science and metaphysics do not have to be autonomous to be meaningfully distinguished from each other. For the person who can

---

5. Consider the following quote: "The attempt to appraise facts objectively and to account for them without distortion . . . should be seen as the difficult task that it is." What are we to make of such claims? "The attempt to appraise facts objectively" is not merely "difficult": it is *impossible*. While the goal of controlling bias is laudable, the claim that bias can be eliminated scientifically is nonsense. Even so, it is a claim often made, or at least inferred, by many contemporary sociologists. (Quoted in Don Martindale, *The Nature and Types of Sociological Theory*. Boston: Houghton-Mifflin, 1981, p. 51.)

distinguish between empirical and value statements, the overlap between the two can be seen as complementary rather than confusing and confounding. Indeed, we must have this overlap—this integration—for science without metaphysics becomes too trivial, and metaphysics without science becomes too speculative.

Continuing our efforts to understand how Christianity and sociology interrelate, we turn in the next chapter to a subject suggested above: *definitional relativity*. By relativity, I mean the various ways symbols of social reality are defined, depending on the social context. In the next chapter, we will see how dependent sociological thought is upon this thesis that social reality is relative and what implications this thesis has for Christians.

3

The Nature of Sociological Thought

Sociologists offer a unique way of looking at the world. Even though there are many distinct theoretical orientations to sociology, all are guided by certain shared assumptions. One is the idea that social reality is multilayered and complex, that there is more to discover than meets the untrained eye. Ever since the discipline got its formal start in European and American universities about one hundred years ago, sociologists have tried to see what others could not (or would not) see: distant and unfamiliar worlds, new ways of thinking and acting, alternative views of our own social reality from vantage points not even imagined by others—views that may make the familiar suddenly seem quite unfamiliar, even strange (Collins and Makowski, 1978).

Skepticism as a Prerequisite

Sociology begins, then, with an awareness that social reality is multilayered—a "debunking" orientation which accepts that there is more to the real world than what one has been taught to think. It begins with a questioning, skeptical attitude, one that seeks to know more than is already known and assumes what is known is somehow incomplete, perhaps faulty.

This debunking orientation is derived from the recognition that social reality is not fixed or unitary. In other words, the way social reality is defined tends to vary from group to group. Each group, in turn, seeks to promote and then accept its own version of so-called reality.

Of course, some groups are better at promoting their own version of reality than others. The groups most successful in convincing others to adhere to their point of view have the greatest influence on what official reality will be. According to Peter Berger, this "official version" of reality never tells the complete story; there is always more to be uncovered. The unmasking of official reality, then, is a chief function of sociology:

> To ask sociological questions . . . presupposes that one is interested in looking some distance beyond the commonly accepted or officially defined goals of human actions. It presupposes a certain awareness that human events have different levels of meaning, some of which are hidden from the consciousness of everyday life (p. 29).

Looking behind the scenes and recognizing that reality is relative is based on a skeptical outlook. It is this skepticism that represents the life's blood of sociological analysis.

Before joining the faculty of the Christian college where I teach, I had a conversation with an alumnus. He asked me about my goals as a professor—what I hoped to accomplish by teaching at his alma mater. I told him that my goals included generating an uncommon degree of skepticism in my students. He paused for a moment, evidently comparing my answer to his memories of the school, and then said, "Perhaps you had better reconsider teaching there. As I remember, skepticism isn't prized too highly."

Regardless of the accuracy of his statement, there ought not be a contradiction between the goals of Christianity and the type of skepticism I try to generate in my classes. However, few of my students appear to agree with me at the beginning of each semester.

The skepticism that lies at the base of sociological awareness is not the same as the cynicism that Christians rightly fear. Cynicism is the attitude that there are no absolute truths—that those who claim otherwise are either stupid or mistaken. Skepticism, on the other hand, is the attitude that the whole truth about reality is not yet known. In short, cynics are people who are convinced that the quest for truth is fruitless, whereas skeptics insist only that our knowledge is incomplete. Skeptics can still believe in the existence of objective truth; cynics cannot. The skeptic and the cynic will often sound as if they are coming from the same position, however, since neither one will claim to know what the complete truth is. Even so, there is a world of difference between the two.

The opposite of skepticism is not sincere belief; its opposite is credulity. Skepticism toward social reality is the predisposition encouraged by Christ and the apostle Paul. Both insist that the social system (that is, the *cosmos*—the world order), insofar as it operates according to evil "principalities and powers," is corrupt, beguiling, and misleading. Christians are warned that the *cosmos* can, if we are not careful, squeeze us into its mold (Rom. 12:2). It is therefore clear from the New Testament that unthinking, gullible conformity to the world system can be dangerous. Christ says that as we lay up treasures here, as we are encouraged to invest in this system and its corruptible goods, we will be steadily drawn away from God's kingdom (Matt. 6:21). So we are advised to be "wise like serpents," aware of the wiles of the *cosmos*. We are told to avoid conformity "to the pattern of this world." Instead, we are to be transformed by the renewing of our minds. It is only then that we will be able to test and approve God's perfect will for our lives.

Since skepticism is characteristic of debunking and relativity, and since both are traits of sociological consciousness, in the remainder of this chapter we will look into the general social conditions whereby skepticism becomes culturally widespread. By doing this, we will also understand the social conditions by which sociological consciousness develops on a wide scale, thereby gaining a measure of insight into the process itself. The assumption here is that those who know more about the *cosmos* are also more likely to gain some control over its influence.

Galileo: A Famous Skeptic

To discover the social conditions in which widespread skepticism arises, let us first consider a period when skepticism was not as widespread as it is now. The era known as the Medieval Age, roughly from A.D. 500–1300, was a time when "official reality" was largely prescribed by the church (headed by the pope), and the state (headed by various kings). Even though some scholars have overemphasized the *darkness* of these times (after all, technological development did not cease altogether, nor did literature and art stop), there was a rather effective effort by political and religious leaders to stifle publicly expressed skepticism. This coalition of groups was largely successful in promoting its version of reality as "the official reality." Many who insisted on a different perspective were labeled heretics, and were treated accordingly.

A classic example of this sort of confrontation was the challenge that an inventor and writer named Galileo Galilei (1564–1642) brought to the then-current view of the physical universe. This confrontation took place long after the close of the medieval period, at a time when scientific investigations were developing rapidly. Even so, the official reality was still powerful enough to make Galileo's skepticism rare.

Among other theories, Galileo questioned whether or not the earth was indeed the center of the universe, something the church had in its public pronouncements declared to be absolutely true. This conclusion tied in logically with the church's beliefs that the earth was the sole locus of human life and that human life was the crowning creative act of God.

Galileo did not keep his questions to himself. As a result, he attracted a rising level of hostility from the gatekeepers of official reality. Using a crudely fashioned telescope, Galileo started making astronomical observations. He discovered mountains on the moon (discrediting the church's position that the heavens were perfect and that irregularity could be found only on the earth, where human sin had presumably corrupted all things). In addition, Galileo discovered that Jupiter was circled by moons, thus demonstrating that the earth was not the center of all heavenly rotation.

Unlike his mentor Copernicus, whose ideas had been published posthumously some fifty years before, Galileo immediately published several pamphlets about his discoveries and theories—a careless (or brave?) act that brought on the charge of heresy. He was officially silenced by Pope Pius V in 1616. Even so, when Pope Pius died and a new pope took his place, Galileo took hope and published *A Dialogue on the Two Chief World Systems,* an act that brought the full wrath of the church down on him. Not only was the book published in defiance of the earlier edict, but it was written in Italian, not Latin, so that any literate person could read it. To cap off the outrage, Galileo fashioned the book as a debate between an able Copernican scholar (Galileo himself) and a bumbler named "Simplicio," whom the new pope (probably correctly) assumed was an insulting caricature of himself.

By now (1632), Galileo was nearly seventy, and having before him the recent example of an unrepentant astronomer who had been burned at the stake, he recanted and made no further publications.

But it was a hollow victory for the conservatives. Galileo's skepticism was based on observations that anyone with minimal training and equipment could duplicate. Neither official sanction nor complicated theological learning was needed to observe that nothing except our moon rotated around the earth.[1]

A New Scientific Perspective Emerges

Very rapidly, a mechanistic model evolved which rapidly demythologized the universe—the same universe previously declared by church officials as wholly sacred and mysterious. Previously, in order to make pronouncements on such heady subjects as heavenly bodies, one had to be theologically trained and have one's learned conclusions legitimated by the church. But this view was increasingly challenged by the radical idea that all one needed to do was study some mathematics, buy a telescope, and have a look. In the process, the church's authority was seriously undermined in the eyes of many intellectuals. If the church fathers were wrong once, they could be wrong again.

---

1. This discussion is based on the account given by Isaac Asimov in his *Biographical Encyclopedia of Science and Technology,* New York: Avon, 1976, pp. 91–96.

Many new scientific insights followed and an alternative view—a new way of interpreting truth—gradually emerged in the seventeenth and eighteenth centuries. Under this new perspective, called "positivism," religion was regarded more as a hindrance to the discovery of valid truth. To lessen the interference of speculative theology, the process of "secularization" was followed; science was kept separate from theology in order to prevent contamination of empirical observation.

The origins of value-free science go back to these positivists. By presumably separating scientific fact from religious value, they attempted to get a clearer picture of the truth and how the world actually works.

A deep irony regarding the development of early science should be noted here. The positivists did not seek to replace the church's truth with a limited, tentative, relativistic so-called truth. Instead, they assumed that scientific truth was both final and absolute. In fact, the type of truth they sought could scarcely be distinguished from the theological truth they had rejected. The positivists sincerely hoped to uncover nothing less than the universal laws of the natural universe by means of the empirical methods of science.

It would take another three hundred years before the hope that science can lead us to final truth would be subjected to the same skepticism that befell religious truth in the seventeenth and eighteenth centuries. The final triumph of relativity occurred in the nineteenth and early twentieth centuries when philosophers, and then scientists, began to turn a skeptical eye on scientific methods and theories.

Meanwhile, it took many centuries for skepticism about the physical universe to develop into an intellectual tradition; but it took considerably more time for sociological skepticism to take similar root. In fact, it did not fully appear until the late nineteenth century—long after physics, chemistry, biology, economics, and psychology had been widely recognized as legitimate scientific disciplines.

In the latter seventeenth and into the eighteenth centuries, men like Hobbes, Rousseau, and Locke started by asking normative questions about the "just society," and the proper role of the citizen in government. It took another century before scholars began to ask truly empirical questions about the nature of social reality. Why is it that skepticism about social reality came so much later than skepticism concerning the physical and natural universe?

The Rise of Sociological Skepticism

In the 1600s, a degree of skepticism could be found, but it was rarely focused on social reality (and if it was, it wasn't done publicly—except, perhaps, in the form of ballads and comic theater). In order to explain why social reality finally became a focal point of scientific skepticism in the late 1800s, we need to examine the process whereby skepticism spreads, and then apply this thesis to the historical illustration just considered.

This discussion is an effort to accomplish two goals: first, to account for the rise in widespread skepticism in the modern world, especially in the form of sociological thought. In other words, I will use sociology to account for its own popularity. Second, by inquiring into the origins of sociological skepticism, I wish to emphasize some of the unique aspects of the sociological perspective. In doing so, the stage will be set in chapter 4 for our discussion of sociological and Christian thought, and how they differ.

For the sake of emphasis and clarity, the analysis is presented in five interrelated parts:

1. Social reality is a complex system of symbols and definitions.

Humans define social reality and act in accordance with these definitions most of the time. Why we do this is a separate matter; the fact before us now is that a social situation (for example, a classroom lecture) is accepted as such only because it is so defined by the participants. Thus, a lecture is a lecture only because those involved define it as "a lecture." If those involved suddenly (and inexplicably) decided to define the situation as a "party," it would *be* a party.

However, note several factors; first, our definitions of reality and our consequent actions are not always in agreement. It is possible to define a lecture as "boring" but act as if it is not. Even so, whether it is boring or not, the situation is still defined as a *lecture*. Second, not all participants in a given situation will have exactly the same definition of what is happening. Most often, however, definitions will be sufficiently similar for the participants to act *as if* they are defining the situation in the same way.

The process of defining reality is not necessarily a conscious or deliberate process. In fact, definitions of reality usually arise without anyone paying much attention to the process at all. Most of us ordinarily accept how reality has been defined by others. Even so, the important point is that social reality is—and must always be—humanly defined.

These statements anticipate the second part of the analysis of how skepticism becomes widespread:

2. *Reality definitions are social rather than individual in nature.*

Definitions of reality are shared. It's not my own subjective and arbitrary definition as to how to employ the English language in writing this book that counts. Rather, the primary factor is the rules of English grammar to which I (largely) conform. We are each awash, as it were, in a river of normative definitions flowing down through history to our present social location. We have learned to accept these definitions (at least most of them, most of the time) to the point where they are incorporated into our subjective consciousness. We learn to think according to these cultural patterns. Even so, the norms continue to have an objective existence; they are external to us— a part of the social system in which we are immersed.

To repeat, social definitions are shared. Social interaction accrues shared meanings as we interact with each other over time. Our actions become predictable and thereby meaningful. We come to expect that others will behave in certain ways in particular situations. Over the course of time, therefore, a shared sense of social reality emerges from the social interaction of the participants. We live within an emergent objective reality that together we (or people like us) have subjectively created. Just as we have inherited most of these reality definitions from the previous generations, so too we pass them on (as best we are able) to the next.

In a sense, then, something more than the sum of the parts is created. A shared reality emerges. This important point about the emergence of the whole from the interaction of the parts can be illustrated with a simple example from biology. If a pond were separated into all of its separate parts—algae here, frogs there, lily pads in this pile, water in those barrels—we would have all the parts but not the pond. Similarly, if I were cut up into my individual parts, Rich Perkins would be lost in the process. In short, when they are reduced to the sum of their parts, biological *systems* are destroyed.

So it is with social systems; whenever people start routinely interacting, something besides the sum total of the individuals results. This extra "thing" is social reality; the subject of sociological analysis. When we speak of a reality that is shared, we imply that it transcends each individual. Consequently, every day each of us deals with a social reality we did not create. But by relating to each other as if the reality is real, we help to sustain it.

Reality definitions are designated as *values* and *norms*. As defined in chapter 2, a value is a general statement of a desired end-state. For instance, if people say that education is worthwhile, they express a value. A norm, however, is a specific expectation for a person in a given situation.

Norms are often related to or derived from values. For example, it is commonly accepted that students in a classroom should be orderly; they should remain in their seats, take notes, raise their hands when they have questions, and so forth. All of these expected actions represent norms—shared expectations of proper conduct. However, the fact that students are in the classroom in the first place is related to the value education has in our society.

Norms and values are not totally binding on every person, nor are they equally binding on all. Regardless of whether or not individuals always adhere to given values and norms, definitions of social reality are nevertheless collectively defined and accepted within all social systems. Therefore, they are part of the social reality studied by sociologists.

3. *Norms and values vary according to certain social factors.*

Two of these factors are variation in *social condition* and *social location*. First, norms tend to change as social conditions change. For instance, contrast the image of the so-called proper male in agrarian societies with that typically found in industrial societies. In agrarian societies, male dominance tends to be a pronounced cultural value. In industrial societies, on the other hand, male/female equality is more likely to be valued. In other words, as we move from one social condition (an agrarian society) to another (an industrial society), values and norms about the proper male tend to change (although they do not change in exactly the same way in every industrializing society).

Values and norms also vary according to social location within a given society. The phrase "social location" refers to how people are placed within a particular system (such as, whether they are rich or poor, male or female, old or young and so forth). A rich, white, middle-aged woman from Atlanta is differently located than a poor, Hispanic youth from the Bronx. Normative expectations accepted in one location are not necessarily those accepted in another location.

The issue of group membership is related to this point. Each group will tend to have its own particular slant on social reality. For example, educated, wealthy Protestants tend to prefer formal church services and sermons that are rational and abstract. On the other hand, poorer Protestants with less education tend to prefer informal services, full of emotionally spontaneous expressions. So, religious norms vary in groups differentiated according to such factors as education and income. In short, so-called proper worship varies by social location.

Generally stated, *reality* varies both between groups and over time. This conclusion has overwhelming empirical support. Remember from the discussion of sociological methods (in chapter 1) that the purpose of sociology is to study reality as it is, not as we wish it to be. Needless to say, this distinction between real and ideal is not easily maintained. Even so, the validity of the social sciences depends upon maintaining this distinction. To assume that our reality is the only legitimate one, and that those who differ from us are inferior in some way represents an attitude that runs contrary to the sociological way of looking at the world.

To be properly understood, every society must be taken on its own normative terms. We learn very little when someone says, "Those people are weird"—only that "they" are different from the observer, and that the observer doesn't like their alternative way of doing things. This tendency to judge other cultures by the standards of our own—called "ethnocentrism"—says more about the subjectivity of the observer than about anything else. Put bluntly, ethnocentrism represents the antithesis of sociological vision.

This point about ethnocentrism leads us to the fourth part of this discussion:

4. People who know only their own group's definitions of reality tend to take these reality definitions for granted.

Accepting culture without question occurs whenever a monopoly on defining reality arises, as in the centuries preceding Galileo.

Persons whose experience is limited to one way of viewing reality (that is, persons who live in "localistic" circumstances) are more likely to "see" reality in a way that is closed to alternative ways of defining it. To be closed to definitional alternatives is called *parochialism*. The greater the cultural monopoly, the more powerful are the social forces that ensure conformity. Under such conditions tolerance for diversity will be limited, and even the ability to imagine alternatives will be reduced. The parochial mind is confined to conventional reality.

By taking social reality for granted, and thus not questioning it, parochial people conform even their imaginations to the existing system. This sort of acceptance is more prevalent among members of societies characterized by a unified or dominant cultural orientation. By contrast, in societies where there are a large number of culturally dissimilar groups coexisting, each with its own interests and definitional slant, any one of the diverse ways of defining reality will less likely be taken for granted.[2]

People who live in such pluralistic situations tend to experience discrepant realities in a marginal way. The marginal person is a person who lives within at least two different worlds.

---

2. This outcome will occur to the degree that the groups interact on a relatively frequent and equal basis. If one group dominates the others and is isolated from them, relativity may not become widespread.

The farmer's son who goes off to the city university, the emigrant to another country, and the missionary, are likely to be marginal in this sense. Unless they have sheltered themselves in some way, they know what it is to live in two or more social realities. Consequently, they experience firsthand the cultural discrepancies that occur. As a result, marginal people are less likely to take one or another reality for granted. What is assumed to be true by parochial people living within a local world may be questioned by those who live marginally. What are seen by some as firm conclusions may be seen by marginals as tentative. Such a perspective probably makes the world a more interesting place in which to live, but it is also a less secure and mentally comfortable world.

The relationship between social location, common experience, and the effects these experiences can have on consciousness are outlined as follows:

Structural Arrangement	Typical Experience	Resulting Orientation
pluralism	marginality	relativity
homogeneity	localism	parochialism

To repeat, persons who know only one set of reality definitions tend to take these definitions for granted. Parochial people (including parochial Christians) do not realize they are viewing life through a fixed lens. Such traditionalists will not usually acknowledge that there are other normal ways of viewing life (other ways—yes: "weird" and "inferior" ways, but not "normal" ways).

5. As marginality becomes widespread, social definitions are defined in more relativistic ways.

In other words, under marginal circumstances, reality definitions tend to lose their taken-for-granted nature.

Conditions that bring about widespread marginality are mostly associated with greater technological efficiency and a more complex division of labor—in a word: modernity. Groups become more numerous and diverse, and as a result, society becomes more pluralistic, social mobility increases the incidence of marginality, enabling the intellectuals (and later the masses) to recognize that social reality is neither fixed nor unitary. This condition generates the skepticism and cultural relativity characteristic of sociological analysis.[3]

In 1721, as European society was rapidly becoming more structurally complex, a philosopher named Montesquieu published a remarkable book entitled *The Persian Letters*. In his book, Montesquieu had Persian tourists travel through France, critically observing and commenting on all aspects of French culture: their politics, diet, religious customs, sexual (mis)conduct, and so forth. The Persians' commentary on French culture and society constituted the text of the book. Of course, it was Montesquieu making the comparisons—critical observations that were in some respects rather scandalous.

Never before had a European published a critical social commentary from an outsider's perspective, comparing in a detached and skeptical way the manners and customs of two different societies. The book was an intellectual bombshell, highlighting the French Enlightenment period. *The Persian Letters* was to the birth of sociology what *A Dialogue on the Two Chief World Systems* had been to astronomy. The books raised fundamental questions about what had been previously taken to be certain knowledge—that French society was "of course" the standard whereby all other cultures must be judged, and that the earth was "of course" the center of a divinely managed universe.

Both books were written at a time of transition, when many influential people wanted to hear something other than the official view, and consequently were willing to listen to the message each author had to offer. However, had both authors lived and written their books a century earlier, respectively, their books would most likely have received little public attention. But their audiences had been cognitively prepared for alternative ways of looking at physical and social reality by their experiences in a rapidly changing world. The old physical and social realities were being challenged by an emerging social

---

3. A brief overview of the development of modern sociological thought is given by David Lyon in his second chapter of *Christians and Sociology* "Sociology of Sociology." A survey of the main sociological concepts provided by Auguste Comte, Karl Marx, and Emile Durkheim is provided, along with a Christian critique of the positivism implied in their theories.

order, and traditional ways of thought were being shaken apart. As a result, an increasing number of intellectuals were willing to admit that all was not yet known, and that what was known was incomplete and faulty. This skeptical orientation has characterized the sciences ever since.

Summary

I started this chapter by observing that "the sociological mind" operates on the basis of a skeptical outlook. Sociologists argue that social reality is multilayered. What is taken for reality varies from place to place and from time to time. Different groups define reality differently. If this much is accurate, then we can begin to understand how official reality represents a sort of facade, masking hidden realities. These alternative behind-the-scenes realities can be recognized only by those possessing a certain quality of mind and the patience and tenacity to take a closer, more careful look at the way the world operates.

This unique style of looking at the world has become widely accepted only within the last century. The purpose of this chapter has been to investigate the social conditions whereby this peculiar style of consciousness arose. The argument designed to reveal these conditions was based upon the following observations and assumptions:

1. Social reality is defined into existence.
2. This definitional process represents a collective (not an individual) effort. Reality definitions emerge from a history of human interaction.
3. These shared definitions of reality (norms and values) vary according to certain features of society, such as different social conditions and social locations.
4. People who are familiar with only one system of reality definitions (and who therefore live within a cultural monopoly) tend to take these definitions for granted.
5. However, as society becomes more pluralistic, marginality increases, producing a social condition that induces widespread cultural skepticism and hence a breakdown in the world-taken-for-granted. It is this skepticism that allows for the development of the sociological perspective.

Debunking and cultural relativity are among the unwritten rules of the sociological game. If one wants to play the game, one first has to learn the rules.

Every good scientist needs to be shown to be convinced. Even so, all good scientists recognize that there are other features of scientific work besides observation. The methods of science are limited, but they are no less significant because of this limitation.

The Rules of Secular Sociology

In developing the argument given here about how and why sociological skepticism arises, I have stirred up a few philosophical questions about the nature of truth and what is meant when we claim a statement is true.

One of the most important of these questions concerns the secular orientation of sociology, an orientation derived from its positivistic origins. Sociologists ordinarily write and talk as if there were nothing other than humans and their doings for them to consider (Vidich and Lyman, 1985). Of course, this limitation to sociological vision is reasonable; we would expect as much from people who are trying to be scientific. "Things human" are assumed to be empirical concerns, while "things extrahuman" (that is, divine) are assumed to be metaphysical concerns.

This conclusion just won't do, for it contradicts itself. The assumption that nature (including humanity) is all that exists is *itself* a metaphysical assumption. In effect, what we have here is a metaphysical position which declares metaphysics off limits.

I am not trying to argue that empirical theory ought to be opened up to include any and all supraempirical forces. That would quickly bring about an end to science. However, I do want to emphasize that Christian sociologists are not the only ones who start from a "speculative" base. All types of sociologists—including the secularists—start with certain metaphysical assumptions. These assumptions inevitably direct and color the theoretical and methodological work that proceeds (Gaede, 1984).

These types of qualifications, however, seem to have been lost from memory. The skepticism characteristic of the sociological perspective has triumphed spectacularly. The all-pervasive skeptical spirit of sociology is the spirit of the modern age.[4]

In the next chapter, I will explore the limits of sociological thought, and the question of how absolutist Christian claims can be contrasted with and related to the skepticism and relativism of sociology.

---

4. Consequently Peter Berger starts his influential book *The Sacred Canopy* with this unqualified declaration: "Society is . . . a human product, and nothing but a human product. . . ." (Garden City, N.Y.: Doubleday, 1969, p. 3).

4

The Problem of Relativity

The sociological perspective is centered on the thesis that social reality is humanly constructed and sustained. Sociology begins with the observation that reality is defined differently in different social situations, that reality can be defined in many ways. The sociological perspective therefore tends toward both skepticism and relativism.

Many orthodox Christians, confronting sociology for the first time, find that these traits do not fit well with the way they have learned to think. Whereas sociologists come at social reality as if it were inherently relativistic, orthodox Christians accept at least certain aspects of social reality as absolute. It is this issue—the contrast between relativity and absolutism—that generates a good deal of the tension between these two ways of looking at the world.

Consider marriage, for example. Every culture accepts a form of the family as normative. However, cultural definitions of so-called proper marriage vary widely according to both time and place. For example, the definitions of proper marriage is a partial function of the technological level of the economy. What is accepted as a good marriage varies from agrarian to industrial

societies, with the former type of society producing a more hier-
archical set of familial roles than those typically found in industrial societies. From a sociological perspective, then, what
constitutes a good marriage is at least a partial function of
where one happens to be when the question is asked.

That's not the only way of looking at the reality of family life,
however. I recently attended a wedding in a nearby evangelical
church. In his remarks to the couple facing him, the minister
emphasized that marriage is not just another arbitrary social
form. Marriage, he said, has been ordained by God, and the
moral principles whereby it operates properly are fixed and
final.

Well, which is it—do norms for marriage vary or are they
universal and absolute?

In this chapter, I will focus on the tensions sociology generates for the "sociologically uninitiated" Christians. I hasten to
add that, in my estimation, the perceived problems are not a
function of a lack of sociological sophistication. There really *are*
some serious problems here—ones that will not dissolve simply
because we become more sociologically sophisticated. Indeed, I
believe just the opposite result is more likely—that, from a
Christian perspective, the more we learn to look at the world in
a sociological way (which, for the vast majority of sociologists, is
a secular way) the more serious these problems become.

I want to make it clear that my purpose here is not to resolve
all the problems between sociological relativism and Christian
absolutism. I will point out what the problems are, but I will not
try to resolve them. Indeed, I do not think they can be completely
resolved in a way that all sociologists and Christians can accept.
Instead, I will analyze the difficulties most Christians perceive
when encountering sociology for the first time; I will try to show
how and why these difficulties develop, and what—if anything—can be said about them. But in the end, considerable
tension between the Christian and sociological ways of looking
at social reality will remain.

Sociological Relativity

To the sociologist, social reality always means so-called reality (that is, reality according to some point of view). What is *true*
here and now may well be *false* there and then.

The conclusion that reality varies according to social context is a pillar of contemporary social scientific theory. Of course, there are multiple theoretical perspectives in sociology and some of them make the relativistic thesis more central than others. Even so, they all incorporate it in one form or another. In fact, a sociologist is as unlikely to reject the relativity thesis as a physicist is to reject the gravity thesis. Every introductory sociology text eventually gets around to claiming (or at least implying) that social reality is neither constant nor universal. After all, the claim is so obviously consistent with the evidence; reality definitions do indeed vary from one situation to another.

However, many sociologists talk and write as if the empirical (and therefore limited) basis of this claim has slipped from their memories. In other words, they routinely extend the conclusion that *"reality" varies* beyond its proper empirical limits, claiming instead that *reality itself varies*.

Before you go on, carefully reread that last sentence and note the following: it is one thing to claim that *definitions of reality* (that is, "reality") *vary;* it is quite another to claim that *reality itself varies*. The first claim—that people accept "reality" differently within different social contexts—is an empirical claim. For example, what was accepted as a good marriage in southern Italy in the 1600s is generally not what is accepted as a good marriage amongst Italian-Americans today. While some definitions have remained essentially unchanged (such as the expectation that the couple ought to have children), many others are radically different (such as the expectation that parents will control their children's choice of marriage partners). To claim that "reality" has remained constant is to ignore the obvious facts of the matter.

By contrast, the second statement—that reality itself varies—constitutes a fundamentally different and more far-reaching claim. Note that the word *reality* has lost its quotation marks. No longer are we referring to how "reality" is defined; now we are talking about what reality really is (and is not). It is asserted that *reality itself varies and is therefore in no way constant*. This bold assertion goes far beyond the limited observation that people define "reality" differently in different contexts. Rather, it is a claim about the nature of reality itself—that there are, in fact, no universal and absolute truths. The claim that *reality varies* is a metaphysical, not an empirical, claim.

Both of these claims can and do give Christians problems. The first conclusion (that "reality" varies) reflects, as I argued in the last chapter, a secular view of the world. Sociologists are oriented toward what humans define as "real" and what humanity has created. It appears that most secular sociologists have little trouble moving beyond the idea that sociology is limited to the study of empirical reality to the idea that empirical reality is all there is.

Christians should object whenever it is suggested that social reality is nothing but a human creation. We believe it is more than that. Yet, as problematic as the first thesis is to Christians, the second thesis (that reality varies) is far more objectionable. As I said before, to conclude that reality varies is also to conclude that there are no absolute and universal truths. This the orthodox Christian will not do.

The problem here should be obvious; people who claim *reality varies* would have to also conclude that Jesus Christ was either mistaken when he claimed to be "the truth" or that he was speaking figuratively (John 14:6). Orthodox Christians would, of course, refute both claims—on the grounds that Christ represents the universal truth of God.

But even from a strictly sociological (that is, a secular and humanistic) perspective there are problems with the thesis. The most important of these is that the metaphysical assertion denying absolute truth is itself a supraempirical claim. Consequently, it has as much scientific support as its opposite claim (the Christian claim that absolute and final truth *does* exist)— that is, none whatsoever.

Even so, many sociologists appear to assume that reality (with no quotation marks) does indeed vary by social context. They go on from this assumption to conclude that any claims to absolute truth must therefore be rejected.

Relativity and Relativism

For convenience sake, I will call this second thesis—the denial of absolute truth—*metaphysical relativism*. According to this argument, all truth claims are products of their respective social contexts. Since social contexts vary, so also does the truth claimed in all contexts. Therefore, the Christian belief in the divinity of Christ is defined as *true* (that is, accepted as "true" in some social contexts but not in others), but certainly not as *true* in *all* contexts—whether accepted as *the truth* or not. A metaphysical relativist would deny such beliefs are equally valid everywhere. Indeed, metaphysical relativists deny that truth exists at all.[1]

Metaphysical relativism must be sharply distinguished from *cultural relativity,* which is the much more modest claim that definitions of "reality" (and not reality itself) vary according to time and place. Sociologists can go out and check whether or not definitions of "reality" do, in fact, vary according to social context. Such studies have been made and the conclusion—long since accepted within the discipline—is that they do. No Christian ought to have the least bit of difficulty with this thesis. (However, as I've said before, the usual secular humanist assumption that humanity represents the *only* creative force *is* problematic to Christians. It is apparently difficult for sociologists to start with the empirical observation that "reality" varies and not somehow wind up with the metaphysical claim that human creativity is all there is to consider.)

Students of sociology who confuse metaphysical relativism with cultural relativity will feel threatened by sociology—and reasonably so.

It is easy to get confused. In fact, many professors of sociology and authors of sociology texts are already quite confused. For example, Ian Robertson, the author of a best-selling introductory sociology text, writes "there is no universal [moral] standard to which we can make appeal."[2] This bold claim, given

---

1. For this reason, metaphysical relativism incorporates ethical relativism—the claim that values are valid only insofar as they are accepted as such. The two forms of relativism—metaphysical and ethical—are closely associated, but they are not identical. The former position claims that truth varies according to social context and that therefore no truth is absolutely *the truth* (that is, valid everywhere regardless of human definition). Orthodox Christians claim that Jesus is the divine Son of God and that this claim is true regardless of whether it is accepted or not. Metaphysical relativists reject all such claims.

The latter position pertains to value claims in particular—that what is morally obligatory in one context may not necessarily be so in another context. Any claim that the Golden Rule, for example, is universally applicable is therefore rejected.

2. The context makes it clear that Robertson is referring to moral standards in this quote (Ian Robertson, *Sociology.* Belmont, CA: Worth, 1983, p. 52). Robertson goes on to say that we would not want to accept everything that has, at one time or another, been

under the auspices of empirical sociology, represents a confused (and confusing) leap from empirical matters to metaphysics (that is, from relativity to relativism). It is a crucial leap I want to analyze.

The argument sociologists like Robertson seems to be making, when stripped down to its essentials, is:

1. Accepted ways of defining reality vary according to social context.
2. "Thinking correctly" consists of conforming to these accepted ways of defining reality.
3. "Thinking correctly" varies according to social context.
4. The definition of correct thinking is therefore not universal.
5. Consequently, it must also be true that anyone who claims that there are such certainties as universal and absolute truths is mistaken.

The first three points represent the essence of "cultural relativity." As I have said before, this position represents an empirical thesis and is consistently supported by sociological research. Students of sociology can make no progress whatsoever in the discipline without first understanding this thesis, accepting its validity, and incorporating it into a general scheme of analysis.

However, in points 4 and 5 there is an unwarranted leap. Here we are told that there are no absolute truths—only relative truths—and that anyone who claims otherwise is incorrect. (As an indication of the leap to come, note that the quotation marks found in point 3 are omitted in point 4.)

But how would one know (in the scientific sense of the word *know*) that there are no absolute truths? This is not an issue

---

considered "acceptable." He rejects, in particular, what the German Nazis did to the Jews. But he doesn't give us any hint whatsoever why we shouldn't accept the Nazis' definitions as equally acceptable to our own. After all, if "there is no absolute standard to which we can make appeal," then isn't everything up for grabs?

In private correspondence, Robertson acknowledges the inconsistency, but claims that an extended discussion of relativity and relativism "would be too complex for introductory students to handle." I disagree; without "handling" the matter adequately all sorts of confusion result.

about which scientists, limited as they are to empirical matters, are qualified to speak with any authority. As I said before, there is no adequate test for this conclusion.

Of course, it would be convenient if we could simply distinguish between "cultural relativity" and "metaphysical relativism," draw empirical limits around sociology (in terms of cultural relativity), and let the matter rest. If we could show that sociology must be limited to cultural relativity, and that it has no proper association with metaphysical relativism, then there would be no sociological threat to the absolutist claims made by orthodox Christians.

Unfortunately, it is not so easy to keep the cultural relativity of sociology properly contained. It seems that whenever we play "the reality game" according to the usual sociological rules, claims to absolute truth are ruled out of order every time. Why?

In responding to this question, I will take two general approaches. First, I will play the sociology game by the rules of secular sociology—assuming that the human perspective on social reality is the proper (indeed, the only) one to take. By taking this perspective, certain problems immediately arise for Christians, the chief one being that confidence in knowing God's absolute truth is seriously undermined. I will try to show why this problem arises, and—within the bounds of secularist sociology—what valuable lessons a Christian student can learn about both sociology and Christian faith.

After playing the game by secularist rules, and emphasizing the problems of such, I will switch to Christian ground rules and see how this switch can affect our perception of the problems encountered between sociology and Christianity.

Secularist Sociology: The Sociology of Knowledge

The source of the problem appears to be what is known as "the sociology of knowledge." Although the sociology of knowledge itself is rarely encountered in introductory sociology courses, its main thesis is always implicitly present.

The sociology of knowledge represents an empirical effort to draw links between what people claim to know and their social context. In other words, the sociology of knowledge is an effort to analyze why different groups define "reality" differently and, in so doing, to show how common patterns of thinking are shaped by social experience. Sociologists who accept this analytical approach assume that "reality" is socially grounded.

In considering the epistemological questions posed by the sociology of knowledge, it is useful to distinguish between the "strong thesis" and the "weak thesis." The *strong thesis* assumes that all knowledge is dependent upon (and is always relative to), the social context of the knower. By contrast, the *weak thesis* assumes that most knowledge is relative, but also that there are some important exceptions to the rule. It is claimed that these exceptions (such as, truths that transcend social contexts) are known by a "cognitive elite"—that is, exceptional people (or people in exceptional circumstances) able to escape the relativities of their social context.

Most of the early sociologists of knowledge were advocates of the weak thesis. Karl Marx proposed such an elite by arguing that those (like himself) who correctly understand "the scientific laws of economics" can know the absolute truth about human history. In a similar manner, Karl Mannheim proposed that members of "the freely suspended intelligentsia" are relatively immune from the effects of their social location.

The weak thesis is generally discredited within contemporary sociology. It is now widely acknowledged that "we're all in this together," and that there is no such thing as a "cognitive elite." The reasons for the greater acceptance of the strong thesis are related to the plausibility of the thesis itself. Within the context of the modern world—which is one of rapid social change, pluralism, and marginality—the plausibility of absolute knowledge and of the existence of "cognitive elites" has eroded. Therefore, as far as most modern sociologists are concerned, there is no credible weak thesis to choose as an acceptable alternative to thoroughgoing relativism.

Assuming, as secular sociologists do, that the weak thesis is not a legitimate option, we are faced with this question: does the strong thesis require the logically consistent person to conclude that truth is inescapably relativistic? Unfortunately for orthodox Christians interested in playing by sociological rules, the answer appears to be *yes*. Sociology appears to be built on a thoroughly secular and relativistic foundation—one that undermines belief in all forms of orthodoxy. Orthodox Christians insist that Christ has created all things and in him all things hold together (Col. 1:15-17). Sociologists recognize no such assumptions as binding on their work as sociologists. To sociologists, reality is humanly created and maintained—*period!* Given these different starting points, is it conceivable that a person could maintain a firm commitment to both sociology and orthodox Christianity? There is no simple yet adequate response to this question. In order to delve deeper into this problem it is necessary to first understand several additional concepts.

Levels of Relativistic Analysis

Human knowledge, said to vary according to social context, can be analyzed on two levels: on a small-scale (within-group, or "microlevel"), and on a large scale (between societies, or "macrolevel"). At the microlevel, sociologists of knowledge examine all forms of knowledge such as are contained in plots, schemes, stories, notions, jokes, clichés, rumors, justifications, rationalizations, instructions, codes, rules, laws (legal and, yes—even scientific), and all other forms of knowledge, to include particular pieces of information (such as, "This is how to turn on the lights in here"). In its jokes and rules, rumors and scientific laws, each group will demonstrate its own accepted ways of defining knowledge—each derived from its own historical experience.

Is knowledge socially located? I don't see how any consistent and informed thinker who accepts the assumptions of sociology could reasonably conclude otherwise. The evidence is overwhelming. All knowledge, it seems, is socially grounded.

Are there any adequate reasons for Christians to be threatened by this conclusion? On one level, at least, I don't think so. For instance, we are given a variety of biblical indications about the tentative and partial nature of human knowledge and its sharp contrast with divine knowledge. For example, in 1 Corinthians 1:25, we read "For the foolishness of God is wiser than man's wisdom. . . ." Yet, although human knowledge is far from perfect, Christians believe we are still capable of connecting with divine truth. Orthodox Christians acknowledge that human knowledge is corrupted, but they do not believe it is thoroughly debased.[3]

Our understanding of God's eternal truth, therefore, is far from complete and fixed. As if to underscore this fact, conservative Christians have been sifting through the Bible for ages, quietly discarding what they interpret to be "outmoded cultural forms," and accepting new ones the Bible doesn't even mention as alternatives. For example, slavery is not condemned in the Bible, but all the Christians I know reject it on moral grounds.[4] Furthermore, I don't know anyone who advocates the stoning of disobedient children or witches, nor do most Christian women I know keep silent in church or cover their heads with a veil.

The list of once-accepted/now-ignored norms could go on and on. Consequently, for Christians to claim that they fully understand God's truth cannot reasonably mean that their interpretations of the Bible are final. Even so, many Christians regularly talk as if they have somehow achieved certainty on a variety of matters.[5]

Such weak-thesis Christian claims appear to contradict some biblical teachings. Consider all those scriptural passages which indicate that "reality" is indeed humanly constructed. For example, Jesus acknowledged our creative capacity when he attacked the religious laws of the Pharisees as nothing more than

---

3. The fact that many Christians appear to be overcommitted to this world's "reality" should not surprise us. Christians have failed at lots of efforts throughout history.

4. True, 150 years ago many Christians didn't see this in the same way, but doesn't this fact support the case I am making here?

5. Fundamentalists (sometimes called "foundationalists," because many assume that "spiritual knowledge" must be absolutely certain or else the whole basis for religious faith collapses) have been playing by these rules for a long time. They simply declare that they have the truth and that those who disagree with them don't.

I will later argue that such foundationalist claims are, ironically enough, inconsistent with what Bible writers themselves claim about divine truth.

Roman Catholics have, of course, dealt with this problem by declaring that the Pope can, in certain matters, articulate the complete truth of God. Martin Luther, after rejecting such papal authority, had to contend with other Protestants who declared their own versions of the truth as final and without error. Luther's comment is, I think, instructive: "If any of you consider your doctrine and theology to be completely true and right, you have only to feel your ears and find that they are the long furry ears of an ass." (Quoted in James W. Shire's "Brave New Publishers: Should They Be Censored?" in *Evangelicalism: Surviving Its Success*, published papers of The Evangelical Round Table: Volume 2, David Fraser (ed.), Princeton: Princeton University Press, 1987, p. 131.)

a set of self-righteous human fabrications. He claimed that some people can be affected by the truth of God, to be sure, but he also recognized that this truth can be ignored or twisted beyond recognition by others. Consider also that Paul declared meat offered to idols was clean, except to people who define the idol as sacred (1 Cor. 8). The critical difference was a matter of human definition. These examples (and many others which could be cited) indicate that human "reality" is constructed, that it is therefore relativistic, and that this relativity is acknowledged by many writers of the Bible as a truth to be incorporated into Christian teachings.

The conclusion shared by both sociologists of knowledge and the writers of the Bible is that social reality, at least as it operates at the microlevel, *is* humanly created and sustained. Consequently, Christians who study sociology for the first time have no substantial reason to be dismayed when they encounter the idea that microreality varies at the microlevel. The real problem appears to lie elsewhere—at the macrolevel of analysis—even though the argument for the relativity of knowledge is the same as the one encountered at the microanalytical level.

When we shift to the macrolevel, we shift to what people accept as "real" in terms of world views. "A world view . . . provides a model *of the world* which guides its adherents *in the world*."[6] Any claim that world views are themselves mere relativistic fabrications ought to concern orthodox Christians deeply. After all, this is the level at which God's Word and the ultimate truths it contains are communicated. The Christian world view sustains knowledge of history's purpose, of the origins and destiny of humanity, our moral basis for social action, the nature of human nature, and so forth. Orthodox Christians do not welcome the news that these truths too are mere human constructions. If relativism must be accepted at this level, then it seems clear that orthodox Christianity is lost.

Before we proceed further, let's look back to see where the argument has taken us. Cultural relativity, as it is ordinarily

---

6. Brian J. Walsh and J. Richard Middleton, *The Transforming Vision: Shaping A Christian World View*. Downers Grove: InterVarsity, 1984, p. 32 (emphasis in the original).

accepted within sociology, tends to expand into metaphysical relativism. This redefinition occurs because the strong thesis has gained a greater legitimacy in the modern world as the plausibility of the weak thesis has been undermined by rapid social change and group pluralism.[7]

It appears, then, that sociologists are left with the strong thesis—and with the idea—that all forms of truth, including ethical truths, are relative to their social context. Put differently, the Christian studying sociology is faced with an argument that appears to lead, however indirectly, to metaphysical and ethical relativism.

Try as we may, as soon as we say that truth varies, we seem to wind up undermining our beliefs in the reality of absolute truth. It is in this way that sociology threatens Christianity. In effect, if one plays the "reality" game by the usual sociological rules, one will wind up hedging on claims to absolute truth. (This is perhaps the chief reason why sociology is not included in the curriculum of Bible schools or fundamentalist colleges, even though psychology, history, and economics usually are.)

In summary then, the strong thesis (and the metaphysical relativism it implies) poses a definite threat. According to this thesis, all forms of truth (and knowledge about truth) vary according to social context, and consequently, knowledge of absolute truth must be denied. Whether or not this conclusion logically follows is unimportant here. The fact is, most sociologists talk and write as if it does logically follow, and most of their students appear to agree.[8]

What's a Christian to Do?

The consistent, secular sociologist will yell "Foul!" whenever anyone (say, a Christian) claims to have an inside track on truth.

---

7. We should not breeze by this point without pausing, as Peter Berger says, "to relativize the relativizers." Metaphysical relativism is itself a cultural definition grounded within a specific historical context. It is an open question, then, just how seriously we should take any truths about "truth," which is itself contextualized.

8. Of course, there is another question here—an epistemological question—"How could we know the absolute truth, assuming it exists?" In other words, does it do us any good to believe absolute truth exists if we frail humans can't possibly know what that truth is?

As I will argue later, sociologically informed Christians are metaphysical absolutists while remaining epistemological relativists.

"Let them yell," says the Christian dogmatist. "God communicates truth to us, and that's all there is to say on the matter." Of course, seen from a perspective which incorporates the sociology of knowledge, any such claim to a cognitive elite status *is* arrogant. What about subjectivity—that is, definition and interpretation? Are not Christians as subject to the currents of history and social context as everyone else? If they aren't, then why have Christians created the various church councils, the creedal statements, Christian denominations, and Bible translations? What of all the theological claims and counterclaims, and so forth? On what legitimate grounds can Christians claim to be a cognitive elite? What does the Christian sociologist have to say to these questions?

Remembering that we are still playing by secularist rules, and without getting caught up in particular details, general responses to these questions can come from two analytical directions: from a *negative* and a *positive* critique of the strong thesis. The first, a negative critique, concerns the self-corrosive nature of the strong thesis as it operates in contemporary sociology. The second response—a positive critique—focuses on how the strong thesis can be bent so as to make it at least appear to be more compatible with Christian absolutist beliefs.

In sum, the negative critique tries to show that Christians aren't the only ones who have serious problems with the strong thesis. The positive thesis attempts to incorporate elements of the strong thesis into what Christians have traditionally believed.

The Negative Critique

First of all, everyone—including the most secular-minded sociologist—needs to recognize the culturally corrosive effects of the strong thesis. What would be the result if everyone were to adopt the strong thesis and conclude that reality does indeed vary? Wouldn't ordinary morality tend to degenerate into mere individual opinion, eventually reaching a state where informal social controls cease to function? As this process occurs (and it is), what can be used to keep self-interest in check: The police? Science? Logic?

Surely we do not want to rely on the police to this extent, for maximizing police coercion comes at the expense of democratic freedoms. Quite clearly, science cannot supply us with moral direction because it is methodologically restricted to empirical questions. And rationality can augment devastating bouts of irrational competition (such as the nuclear-arms race).

Where then does all this leave us? If we can show that the widespread acceptance of relativism is socially destructive, and that sociology is one of its carriers, shouldn't sociologists—no matter how secular their personal orientation—be concerned? By implicitly denying the necessity of moral consensus, do we not open wide the gates to eventual chaos?[9]

Analyzed this way, it is possible that the strong thesis actually contributes to the breakdown of social order. (It is certainly not the chief factor producing this result. Here, sociology is more a symptom than a cause.) To the degree this argument has validity, we can conclude that sociology helps to destroy its own subject matter—a regrettable outcome, most would agree (Bendix, 1971).

There does seem to be a problem in all this for those who advocate the strong thesis, but—admittedly—there isn't any logical inconsistency. Pointing out the potentially corrosive effects of sociological thought does not, in itself, undercut the strong thesis on either logical or empirical grounds. There may be some practical inconsistency, and adherents of the strong thesis ought to own up to the inconsistency more than they do, but these claims amount to little more than an *ad hominem* attack and for this reason alone is not likely to convince the skeptics.

Yet, there are still other reasons why sociologists ought not get too comfortable with ethical relativism. For example, every sociologist acknowledges that a thoroughgoing ethnocentric orientation represents the annihilation of the sociological perspective. Yet at least one problem involving values immediately pops up when we make this claim: to declare another culture "ethnocentric" is, in itself, evidence of an ethnocentric orientation! If

9. Of course, liberals and radicals, both of whom have a cheerier view of human nature than is implied here, will disagree with my pessimistic prediction.

we are to be consistently relativistic, then who are we to declare our cosmopolitan sociological perspective preferable to the ethnocentrism of others? Are we not implicitly claiming our perspective as universally normative? And if relativistic sociologists were to back off and refuse to declare ethnocentrism to be sociology's enemy, then does not the discipline lose its basic reason for existence?

Perhaps some will respond by saying that the sociological opposition to ethnocentrism is not, in itself, evidence of otherwise relativistic sociologists unaccountably resorting to absolutes. Perhaps, they will say instead that it is simply a matter of ranking one value (such as being openminded) over another (such as being logically consistent). If so, however, can they say on what evaluative basis this ranking is accomplished? Why is the one value given priority over the other?

In addition, the strong thesis has problems because it extends itself beyond the empirical limits of sociology. It has been clearly demonstrated that people (Christians, of course, included) are influenced by their social environments. This much has been empirically demonstrated. However, it has not been demonstrated that people are entirely unable to transcend this influence. Indeed, if it had been demonstrated that people are unable to overcome the effects of their social contexts, then what could we make of the thesis itself? Would not it too be seen as a product of mere social circumstance (and dismissed accordingly)?

It appears, then, that the strong thesis undermines itself. Its conclusion (that is, metaphysical relativism) constitutes, ironically enough, an absolute claim to truth. In effect, the strong thesis appears to claim that it is absolutely true that no absolute truths exist. If this is a contradiction (and it certainly appears to be such), then not many sociologists I know seem to be bothered by it (Moberg, 1962).

Thus, I have tried to show that orthodox Christians aren't the only ones who ought to find metaphysical and ethical relativism problematic. Of course, this conclusion doesn't neutralize the problems Christians face from sociologically induced relativism, but it does show that they have lots of company—secular sociologists among others.

My point in the preceding section has been to show that sociologists cannot afford to fully embrace the thoroughgoing relativism of the strong thesis. In the next section, I will argue that Christians cannot afford to ignore it either. Like it or not, we must come to grips with this thorny matter, or else give up some of our claim to intellectual integrity.

The Positive Critique

The Christian's rejection of the strong thesis is based on the assertion that all "mentally functioning adults" can adequately understand the gospel, God's universal and final truth, regardless of cultural context.

Of course, simply to make this claim does not undermine metaphysical relativism. As I stated at the beginning of this chapter, I do not intend to show that Christian absolutism and sociological relativism can be fully reconciled. Even so, I think it is possible to show that the difference between the two perspectives does not amount to a clear-cut contradiction.

Social reality is symbolic. Sociologists say that this symbolic reality operates as "an illusion" because it is humanly constructed and because it therefore varies by social context. However, can't we meaningfully distinguish between the symbols and the "underlying reality" itself? Are there not universal realities—whatever their level of existence (i.e., their ontological status)—that can be distinguished from the symbols themselves? For example, fear, anger, love, forgiveness, loyalty, embarrassment, all appear to be universal. True, the cultural symbols of each do vary, but some or all of the meanings are universal. When embarrassed, Okinowans tend to smile and giggle. When faced with a similar situation, North Americans typically frown or blush. The symbols of embarrassment—giggling and blushing—vary; the embarrassment is, I presume, constant.

When analyzing "reality" and how it does or does not vary, we ought to identify the levels of reality with which we are concerned. Are we interested in the symbols, the "reality" they represent, or perhaps some yet deeper structures of human consciousness and linguistic expression not yet mentioned? In other words, despite the fact that cultural symbols do vary, the underlying structures of social life may be sufficiently universal to be capable of conveying the gospel story into the symbols of every cultural system. The elements of the gospel story—the fall from created perfection, divine sacrifice, reconciliation, and salvation—are, I assume, found in all symbol systems. The fact that the symbols of perfection, evil, sacrifice, and salvation vary from culture to culture isn't all that important. Christians can communicate transcendent truths despite all the evidence of cultural relativity. Social-scientific studies demonstrate that humans are biased. Yet everyone is not equally biased. Similarly, even though sociologists assert that all "realities" are socially defined, it does not follow that all aspects of every social reality are equally relative. For example, the idea that "bank loans will be set at 11.25 percent interest" is a mutually agreed upon human fiction useful for the purpose of monetary exchange within a limited social context. But the idea that "one is obligated to show special consideration to one's friends" is not a "mere fiction" in the same sense; it reflects a moral standard found, in one form or another, in every society. The relativity of bank loans sharply contrasts with the universal injunction to be loyal to one's friends (Lewis, 1943).

In sum, to admit that "reality" varies doesn't have to imply that there are no cultural universals. In response to the challenge of relativism, Christians claim that the gospel is universally applicable—that it is relevant to every culture (and on each culture's own terms) without losing its essential truthfulness.

Those who believe in God's truth have long accepted the thesis that relativity and absolutism are not necessarily contradictory. How else could Christians claim that Christian conversion results in the redefinition of key aspects of "reality" (1 Cor. 1:18). Moreover, Christians accept that humans "see through a glass darkly." To say this much is not the same as to say we see nothing at all. In short, the writers of the Bible acknowledge that "reality" varies, yet they do not push their relativity to the point of relativism.

One other point: that our Christian world view may, in fact, be socially located isn't in itself a valid reason to regard orthodox claims as necessarily false. In other words, our Christian beliefs about the world may be objectively true, even though a plausible case can be made for their social grounding. After all, the sociological claim that slavery ended due to the growth of industrial capitalism doesn't alter the validity of the moral claim that slavery is morally wrong and that it should not be reinstated.

What to Do

If the above arguments do not successfully neutralize the threat from the strong thesis of the sociology of knowledge, there are still several viable compromises. In effect, Christians can acknowledge the validity of sociological relativity and still maintain that humans have access to God's truth.

At the macrolevel, concerning the sweep of world history, Christians have always believed that God's truth works its way through the structures of history. In fact, this claim is close to that made by one of the founders of the sociology of knowledge, Max Scheler (*see also,* Gaede and Clark, 1981).

At the micro-analytical level, Christians can acknowledge the validity of the relativistic thesis and make it work for them. They can accept the validity of the sociological thesis by choosing to get themselves into a social location where the gospel can be more fully and properly understood (Rom. 5:3, 4). If God's kingdom is coming to the poor and oppressed, as Jesus declared early in his ministry (Luke 4:18, 19), then perhaps it would be a good idea to become poor and oppressed. Grasping this insight, affluent Christians could elect to give up their privileged status and identify directly with the oppressed—in fact, identifying to the point of actually joining up. In this way, they could experience the gospel from a new perspective more consistent with Jesus' declaration. (We can expect the level of enthusiasm with which affluent Christians will greet this suggestion to be equal to that displayed by the rich young ruler who was told by Christ to sell all he owned: Luke 18:18–30.)

By electing to alter our social locations so as to attain a different basis of understanding, we acknowledge a central sociological claim: that experience sets the context for awareness. If this suggestion is appropriate, we could conclude that sociological relativity is actually an asset for those earnestly pursuing the kingdom of God.

Recall how often Christ declared that not all who have ears to hear would understand the truth. Did not Christ declare that those who would enter the kingdom of God must first turn aside from everything in order to follow him? Our problem, it seems, arises less from sociological relativism and more from our reluctance to take Jesus seriously.[10]

After all the arguments are summed up—that is, the self-contradictory nature of relativism (the negative critique), and the Christian's acknowledgement that a proper understanding of the gospel is influenced by one's social location (the positive critique)—there still doesn't seem to be logical closure on this perplexing issue. No matter how we try, we can't seem to reach absolutism from a relativist/empirical basis, or vice versa. The best that can be done is to show how the two positions—secular sociology and orthodox Christianity—are not as far apart as many think. We can then make an estimate of where the arguments and counterarguments take us, and leave the matter there.

Thus the strong thesis appears to survive. What, then, is a Christian who wants to understand "things sociological" to do? Many Christians, recognizing the threat sociology poses, advise us to avoid sociology. Others segregate their religious beliefs from their sociological knowledge. I try not to do either. Instead, *we ought to pay serious attention to sociology, and learn to live with the tension.*

After all, whoever said life could (or even should) be lived without tension? If there ever was a group prepared to live with significant tension, it ought to be Christians. We are the ones who believe we must be *in* but not *of* the world. We believe that we make decisions directing the course of our lives, yet do we not also believe that God is in control of history? We claim we are saved by grace, not by our works, yet we also do good works as a sign of our salvation. We acknowledge that salvation is always personal but never individual; that Christians are dead in sin yet alive in Christ; that we lose our lives in order to find them; that humans are both good and evil; that Jesus was both God and man; that the meek inherit the earth; that we live in a natural world, yet we witness miracles; that God is three persons in one,

---

10. John Alexander, *Your Money or Your Life*, New York: Harper and Row, 1987.

and that God has always existed, even though there is nothing in our experience that confirms such a belief.[11]

How's that for tension? As Christians, we are asked to believe sets of ideas that cannot be fully reconciled. Consequently, living with tension and paradox ought to be old hat for orthodox Christians. I ask only that we add yet another paradox to the already impressive list: that Christians believe in the reality of God's truth, yet acknowledge that humans must always interpret it as "truth."

In the face of all these tensions, we need to keep in mind that "the only thing that counts is faith expressing itself through love" (Gal. 5:6b). By quoting this verse, I do not wish to downplay the problem of relativism or the importance to orthodox Christians of claiming a relationship to God's truth. Even so, the Christian's main concern ought never to be focused on how certain we can be about our knowledge of God's truth, but on maintaining our faith, despite all the uncertainties. To stress the certainty of truth (from a human perspective) is to run the risk of supplanting faith with another human idol—our own cognitive perfection. This heresy is common enough in evangelical circles, given the propensity of modern-day conservative Christians to emphasize propositional truth, and in so doing, to continue the errors of old-time positivism under another name.

It is indeed ironic to note how those who most vehemently emphasize being separated from the *cosmos* are so often conformed to its image.[12]

---

11. I say none of this in order to encourage those Christian irrationalists who claim that, since human wisdom equals God's foolishness, that we have warrant to maximize our foolishness. Spiritual liberation is not found in the idiocy of free-wheeling self-contradiction. We do not sustain Christian truth by believing contradictory claims (e.g., that we have sinful natures, but we can also have certain knowledge). We need to recognize the paradoxes of truth, but this is not the same as believing theories that could not possibly be true. For, as Freud once asked, if we are to believe one absurdity, why not believe them all?

12. The pronouncements of some evangelicals on the matter of truth sound more like the effusions of nineteenth-century positivists than orthodox Christians. Consider this claim by Miles Stanford: "True faith must be based solely upon Scriptural facts. . . . Unless our faith is established on facts, it is no more than conjecture, superstition, speculation, or presumption. . . . Once we begin to reckon (count) on facts, our Father begins to build us up in the faith." In short, in the words of Alexander R. Hay, "Faith must be based upon *certainty*" (*Principles of Spiritual Growth*, Back to the Bible, n.d. pp. 7–9).

Playing the Game by Christian Rules

Our discussion of the tensions between relativistic sociology and absolutist Christianity would be far from complete if I did not point out that Christian sociologists can play the reality game by different rules. As I stated in the last chapter, secular sociologists usually operate as if all we need to concern ourselves with is the humanly constructed social order. The natural world is assumed to be a closed, self-initiating, self-perpetuating world. If we play by these rules, then the Christian will inevitably be sucked into the problems of relativism. The principal question, then, is this: if social reality is humanly created (and *only* humanly created), then how can Christians rightfully claim to know God's truth?

Well, we can't.

But this answer begs the question of our priorities; should we Christians play the sociology game according to secularist rules? Should we assume, as secularists do, that human creativity is all we can rightfully consider in our study of reality? Should we assume before we begin that there are no absolute truths to be considered? If we do, then the argument is stacked against the Christian from the start and secularist conclusions are insured. We Christians lose every time when we play by these rules.

To be a Christian sociologist, however, is to play by different rules. Instead of assuming the origins of social reality are exclusively human, Christians assume that the essential features of reality have been divinely ordained. This situation is not merely a matter of playing quick and easy with the rules of empirical sociology—declaring a miracle, or some other "irrationality," whenever it is convenient ("I know I can't grasp absolute truth as a human; the fact that I do is simply a miracle"). This sort of fast footwork will not do. If we allow ourselves this sort of out, we may as well give up logic and science altogether and dive directly into mysticism. Instead, Christian sociologists need to remain loyal to empirical methods and the rules of logic, but they also need to be among those who recognize that all empirical theory rests on a metaphysical foundation. So, while the secularist talks of "nature," the Christian talks of "creation." According to Christians, God created humans in the divine image—that is, as a creator (a free agent) and as a social being. Human rebellion against God's law brought sin into the world—sin being, among other factors, the source of bias (and hence relativity). Bias is also the reason humans are now incapable of fully grasping God's perfect truth. Nevertheless, just as by faith secularists declare human creativity and "truth" to be all there is, so too, by faith, Christians assert the opposite—that God's truth is real, and that by divine initiative it impacts on human history. Accordingly, Christians believe that knowledge and ethics are not completely relative—that the truth of the gospel relates to all cultures and that it endures to all generations.

Christian sociologists will readily acknowledge that all these assumptions are "metaphysical" in nature, *but they are no less metaphysical than the assumptions underlying secular sociological theory.* For sociologists to dismiss "Christian sociology" as "mere metaphysics," and secular sociology as "scientific" is not only naive, but arrogant.

Seen in this way, human bias and subjectivity does not pose the serious obstacles they do to the positivistic version of Christianity, with its built-in definitions of truth as exclusively propositional and rational. Rational knowledge is one tool in the Christian's workroom, but it isn't the only one. Furthermore, rationality isn't primarily what the writers of the Bible had in mind when they spoke of apprehending God's truth.

Christianity has never been simply a matter of accepting a list of propositions as *true.* Indeed, the center of Christian truth is Christ, who proclaimed himself as that truth. The Roman governor in charge of Christ's trial, attuned as were all educated Romans to propositional truth, asked Jesus, "What is truth?" The answer to his question stood right in front of him, but since Pilate heard no rational response, he assumed the question had not been answered. Like many of our own contemporary rationalists (many of them Christians), Pilate couldn't understand and accept truth in the form of a person, nor as a vital ongoing personal relationship.

None of us would think to devalue the understanding parents have for their children because it is so "subjective." We Christians should willingly acknowledge the subjectivity of our relation to divine truth. Indeed, we need to assert that our subjectivity is a crucial element, just as it is in all relationships. The type of knowledge Christians have of God is dependent upon the relationship we have with Jesus Christ—the Word of God. In loving my wife, I know certain facts about her—her age, birth date, eye color, and so forth. But my essential knowledge of her comes from the experience of loving her. Accordingly, grasping the truth of the gospel is not simply a matter of comprehending a set of facts, like learning that 2 x 2 = 4. To know God's truth is to engage oneself in the gospel story—a story that any child can understand. It is to become personally involved in that story—becoming a character in the plot, so to speak. As the story unfolds and engages us, we are increasingly willing and able to grasp its truth.

Summary

Christian sociologists acknowledge that from a human standpoint, all our knowledge is both relative and incomplete—including our understanding of divine truth. *Yet we believe, through faith, that God's truth expressed in the gospel prevails despite our fallen and corrupt condition.* This understanding is a matter of faith enacted in love—of committed belief lived out in personal relationship with the truth. Therefore, to the Christian, human subjectivity and absolute truth are not contradictory.

Christians need not seek certain knowledge. Rather, we should seek to become personally involved in the gospel story and in the relationships reflective of God's truth found within the earthly kingdom of God.

So, tensions between absolute truth and our relativistic grasp of that "truth" will persist, but such tension should not be defined as contradictory—as it is within both overrationalized Christianity and secular sociology.

Looking Ahead

Later I will show that the tension generated between sociology and Christianity can actually work to the Christian's advantage. First, however, we will turn our attention, in Part 2, to a topic that is central to the discussion of relativity in sociology—the issue of how Christians have taken on characteristics connected more to their social locations than to the gospel story. The central focus in Part 2 is on the topic of ideological commitments.

Ideologies are integral to the examination of both Christianity and sociology, although adherents of both perspectives often deny this. After discussing the nature of ideologies and their effects, we will then be in a better position to understand the contribution that sociology can make to Christians. Our central focus will be on the ways in which Christianity has become integrated into the structures and cultural patterns of society, the *cosmos*. In looking into this process through sociological eyes, we will seek to understand how orthodox Christianity has lost some of its original purpose and character. By acquiring sociological insights on the matter, we will see how such insights can help us become disengaged from the *cosmos*, and in so doing, establish a right relationship with God's truth.

Part 2

Looking at the Problem of Ideology

In chapters 1 and 2, we saw how sociology draws on the heritage of scientific inquiry, acquiring both the promises and the limitations of that heritage. We continued by discussing how sociology focuses its scientific skepticism on social reality, examining how a collective sense of reality is created, maintained, and changed. The major theme of chapter 3, a basic insight of sociology itself, is that people define social reality as their experience is shaped within their social contexts. Therefore, sociologists say that "reality" (that is, reality as it is defined) varies according to social location—a thesis that introduces cultural relativity and its troublesome philosophical variants, metaphysical and ethical relativism.

In chapter 4, we examined the challenge that sociological relativity presents to orthodox Christians. I argued that since human interpretation is inescapable, and because interpretation is relative to one's social context, that absolute and universal truth is, there-

97

fore, from a human standpoint, elusive—justifying the centrality of faith over certainty in Christian (and scientific) thought.

The key theme of Part 1 is this: Sociology is built on a secular, humanistic foundation—one that needs to be closely and critically examined by Christians. While the skepticism of the sociological perspective is compatible with Christianity, this compatibility has limits. Christians (that is, orthodox Christians) reject the assumption that human creativity is all that exists and/or matters, as well as the operating assumption that absolute truth does not exist.

In these ways, Christianity serves as both a check and a corrective to what Christians see as the false metaphysical base of contemporary sociology. In so doing, the secular metaphysical foundation of sociology can be rehabilitated in terms consistent with biblical Christianity. We do not have to continue playing the game of sociology by ordinary secular rules.

Even so, it is a mistake for Christians to dismiss sociology out of hand (as is too often the case). I realize that the overall tone of Part 1 is critical of sociology, yet I remain an enthusiastic supporter of the sociological perspective. To demonstrate this support, I want to turn and face another direction in Part 2; I want to show how the sociological perspective can be a valuable addition to the analytical repertoire of contemporary Christians. In particular, I will show how the sociological perspective can help Christians understand who we are, how we got that way, and what we can do about it.

In Part 1, we focused on the problems that sociological relativism poses for Christians as it arises out of constructionist sociology. In Part 2, I want to introduce and explore another important source of tension between Christianity and sociology—the ideological disparity existing between conservative Christianity and "structuralist" sociology. Central to (but somewhat implicit in) these ideological differences are various definitions of freedom and determinism. These differing definitions are products of metaphysical assumptions about the nature of society—in particular, the assumption that society does or does not represent the sum of its parts. The American middle-class value of individualism (in particular, the assumption that society represents nothing more than the sum of its parts) consistently leads orthodox Christians in an ideologically conservative direction—one which conflicts with the way most sociologists tend to define society. Furthermore, in their acceptance of individualism as a central value, conservative Christians have interpreted the gospel as largely a matter of correct doctrinal belief and personal piety.

In the first chapter of this section, chapter 5, rudiments of ideological thought are set out, identifying the parameters of conservative and radical assumptions. I discuss the divergent claims made by each end of the ideological spectrum concerning justice, freedom, and equality. The key aspect of this chapter is to highlight the connection between ideological conservatism and the value of individualism.

In addition to being an important sociological concept (worthy of consideration in its own right), ideology has been an important factor in the development of North American evangelicalism. There is an irony in this development, since evangelicals have always insisted that their ultimate authority is the Bible. I think it can be shown, however, that the gospel message has been combined with certain ideological themes consistent with middle-American values and beliefs. In particular, evangelicalism represents the gospel as filtered through a set of individualistic assumptions. In so doing, that message has been substantially altered in an ideologically conservative direction.

The connections between conservatism, individualism, and evangelicalism will be explored, using the sociological perspective sketched in Part 1.

The sociological perspective attempts to connect the thoughts and acts of particular persons to their respective social locations. One aspect of this perspective (the social location of thought) has already been explored in chapters 3 and 4. In chapter 6, the focus is on the structural orientation characteristic of sociological analysis. Not all sociologists emphasize to the same degree the ways social structures channel thought and action. Even so, sociologists can be counted on generally to argue that we reflect the structures in which we are located. The collectivistic orientation of sociology is contrasted and compared to the individualistic focus of conservatives in general, and conservative Christians in particular.

Using several examples of social research, we will extract two separate questions that need to be asked about social action. One concerns why particular individuals think and act as they do. The other concerns the nature of group interaction, and why patterns of action and thought tend to differ from one group to another. I will argue that each type of question must be asked and then answered in terms consistent with its own analytical approach.

The collectivistic perspective of structural sociology challenges (and rightly so) the individualism characteristic of many contemporary evangelicals. As a result, sociological analysis seems culturally unfamiliar and, yes, even threatening.

Some of this threat emanates from the ideological baggage piled onto American evangelicalism over the past one hundred years. The purpose of chapter 7 is to examine some of the ways evangelical Christianity has accumulated this cultural baggage and to underscore the ways a sociological perspective can help Christians gain some needed "cognitive distance" from it. In chapter 8, this line of analysis is continued by distinguishing between problems pertaining to individual morality and those pertaining to social structures. I criticize ideologically conservative Christians for neglecting the proper study of social structure, and structuralist sociologists for writing as if personal character and morality are irrelevant to the operation of social systems.

5

How Ideologies Work

This person says private property is a fundamental right because each owner's labor is invested in it. That person says private property is wrong because it tends to divide us into contesting classes, generating serious conflicts. Both repeat ideas first uttered by philosophers long since in their graves.

Most likely, these two contemporaries do not consider themselves ideological advocates. Perhaps they wouldn't even recognize the philosophers' names if someone mentioned them. No matter, the ideas live on.

Ideologies are important. Our ideological commitments influence how we interpret policy, help us estimate the worth of persons, guide us in determining whether we have been treated fairly or not, and so forth; yet few Americans appear to know very much about ideologies. This ignorance is a problem because, as citizens of a republic, we ought to be familiar with ideologies—their form and functions—if for no other reason than greater awareness can lead to more knowledgeable involvement in public debate.

For the Christian, there are other reasons why awareness of ideological issues is important. The more we understand ideologies, the more we can control their inescapable effects on how

101

we interpret social reality. Awareness is desirable because the Christian who knows the least about ideologies is the Christian who will most likely be controlled by them. As already noted, in Romans 12:2 we are warned against letting the world system (the *cosmos*) squeeze us into its mold. Instead, we are to "be transformed by the renewing of [our] mind."

One of the most important ways that the *cosmos* shapes our thinking is by ideological means—particularly those ideologies that are so familiar that they become taken for granted. If we claim—as most Christians do—that our highest ideal is to have the Word of God influence our decisions, then it will be necessary to examine our ideological claims more carefully than is usually the case.

The purpose of this chapter, then, is to increase our understanding of ideologies, thereby creating the possibility for greater control over their effects. In raising these issues, I will also be setting up the argument which follows in the next two chapters. As will be shown in chapters 6 and 7, many contemporary evangelical Christian beliefs serve ideological functions. While Christians cannot expect to remain free from all ideological influences, we can seek to gain greater analytical distance from them. We can begin to do this by considering how ideologies are formed and how they become part of our thinking process. In this way, we can gain greater awareness of the process, and in so doing, increase our control over its effects, thus gaining a measure of freedom—not from ideologies, but over the ideological choices we make.

Inequality and Legitimacy

People do not attempt complex and morally questionable tasks without thinking up some pretty good reasons for doing so. Building up and defending an empire, stabilizing a new government, going off to war, restructuring the tax laws, and so forth, all require (and usually get) elaborate justifications. Ideologies do precisely this; they consist of beliefs which help to explain and justify a way of doing something controversial. By contrast, ordinary and simple conventions (like driving on the right side of the road or telling time on a twelve-hour clock) usually do not require deliberate justifications. Other conventions, however, which could be or are questioned by groups with antithetical interests are intentionally legitimated—that is, defined as morally proper—by means of ideological argument.

In most cases, sociologists use the term *ideology* to refer to widely shared beliefs and values used to legitimate systems of distributing goods unequally.[1] Generally speaking, the goods divided unequally are types of privilege, power, and prestige. Social structures arise by which these three categories of goods are routinely and systematically divided in terms of social, political, and economic institutions, respectively.

Ideologies defend structured ways of unequally distributing these goods. Thus we have social ideologies, such as racism and egalitarianism; economic ideologies, such as capitalism and socialism; and political ideologies, such as totalitarianism and representative democracy. There are, of course, many variations within each category, but all attempt to explain and justify a given method of distributing goods unequally. In other words, every ideology represents the desire to convert comfort and convenience into correctness.

Ideologies and Interests

Each ideology, then, represents an attempt to define "reality" so as to perpetuate a group's vested interests. The group's vested interests are derived from its social, political, and/or economic goals. We would expect, therefore, some of the vested interests of labor unions to differ sharply from those of corporate management. Whereas one group seeks to raise wages and fringe benefits, the other seeks to lower production costs. These two sets of interests do not always conflict, but they usually do. Differing interests account for different ideological commitments which, in turn, are used to justify opposing demands, such as those made during collective-bargaining sessions.

Ideologies provide ready-made answers to life's difficult questions. They give us clues as to how to properly define specific behaviors in differing situations. They help us distinguish good

---

1. Ideologies aren't always conservative. They can also be used to attack the legitimacy of an existing system. Sometimes these "attacking ideologies" are called "utopias." Here I will use *ideology* to refer to both types.

guys from bad guys; they help us to clarify the difference between what is true and what is false; who makes sense and who
is off the wall.

Often, an ideology can become so dominant and pervasive
that it functions as a set of ready-made answers to questions
rarely asked. In other words, ideologies play a crucial role in
establishing the world-taken-for-granted. Should it happen,
however, that such questions are asked, they usually receive "of
course" answers. Is private property good? Of course! Are freedom fighters justified in their attacks? Of course! Are terrorists
pursuing evil ends? Of course!

How can we make sense of the muddle of ideological debate?
How can we sort through all the complex claims and counterclaims? First, we can do ourselves a major favor by eliminat-
ing from consideration what might be called "ideologies of
convenience." Here I refer to those spur of the moment ideological claims made by people who have an interest in maintaining any temporary advantage.

When my two children were small, they often played checkers. When they did, they inevitably argued over the "gotta-
jump" rule. One day Dave would insist that "kings gotta jump,"
whereupon Kristina would hotly insist that the rule didn't apply. The next day the situation would likely be reversed, with
Kristina now insisting that Dave had to jump her piece with his
king.

It doesn't take a sociologist to figure out that both children
usually argued in favor of their own circumstantial (and thus
temporary) interests. The general guideline in checkers (as in so
many other situations) is: if the rule helps you to win the game,
apply the rule!

Ideological arguments are often like this. It is a simple function of what we might call "the checkers phenomenon." The
same person might be antiabortion, ambivalent on civil rights,
pro-handgun registration, and anticapital punishment—not
because of any consistent ethical or logical principle lying behind these separate ideological positions, but because that person's immediate interests are served in each particular case.
And if one's interests change (to include the friends one must
please in the course of ordinary conversation), we can expect a
convenient ideological shift to follow.

Some of this checkers phenomenon goes on at rather lofty levels. Much of the disagreement over the nuclear-arms debate between the USA and the USSR is of this sort. For example, for the purpose of arms reduction, the negotiators for the USA want to count only U.S. missiles, whereas the Soviet negotiators want to add in the missiles of America's European allies. The reasons for these different perceptions of what is "fair" are easy to figure out. The differences do not arise from general philosophical differences but from interests that fluctuate as one's political goals shift around. Therefore, what is "crucial" on Tuesday may be "insignificant" on Thursday.

In what follows, I will ignore the checkers phenomenon and will center instead on more complex (and consistent) matters.[2]

Conservatives and Radicals

We can begin our analysis of ideologies with the well-known differences between ideological *conservatives* and *radicals*. First, we will identify the common assumptions underlying these ideological extremes. These differences, originating from various assumptions regarding human nature and the social order, are summarized in figure 3.

As the chart indicates, radicals begin by assuming that human nature is either "benign" or "good." That is, given the "right" kind of social order (that is, one that is noncompetitive), humans will naturally seek altruistic ends and thus the collective good. Radicals tend to think that if people are competitive and selfish, it is because they live within a society where selfishness is demanded and rewarded. Such systems are defined as "oppressive" and ought to be replaced.

By contrast, starting with a much less optimistic picture of human nature, conservatives seek to preserve the existing system which keeps its naturally uncooperative members in check. Conservatives the world over have a rather dark view of human nature. Conservative Soviets, Argentines, Chinese, and North

---

2. I refer, then, only to the analysis of ideological commitments made by intellectuals. These are the people who systematize ideologies for others. To most everyone else, ideological claims are often little more than a hodgepodge of mutually contradictory assertions. Ideology works at this level, but it does not usually represent a system of any sort.

Fig. 3   **Common Characteristics of Radicals and Conservatives Within All Stratified Societies**

| | Responses That Typify Ideologists as: | |
Ideological Issues	*Radicals*	*Conservatives*
Regarding the nature of human nature:	optimistic, altruistic	pessimistic, selfish
If unconstrained, people will naturally:	pursue collective welfare	pursue selfish interests
View of existing system of social controls:	evil/oppressive; needs to be replaced	good/necessary; conserve it
The present social system is therefore:	oppressive at worst, unnecessary at best	good at best, necessary at worst
Basic need taking priority over all others:	need for personal fulfillment	need for social order

Americans all agree that people are born with selfish inclinations. It's the social system that presumably keeps them from each others' throats.

However, the ideological picture is a good deal more complex than this. Nations can also be divided up into various ideological categories, the most general being "liberal" and "illiberal" types. "Liberal" nations (such as, Western democracies) feature individual social, political, and economic rights, and provide them legal protection. The word *liberal* comes from the Latin verb "to free." Since the time of the Enlightenment, the word *liberal* has referred to the general assumption that the basic unit of each society is the individual citizen. Each citizen enjoys certain fundamental rights of citizenship, which include the right to influence the government and its laws. It is from this classically liberal view that we get Thomas Jefferson's familiar claims that "all men are created equal" and that they are all "endowed with certain unalienable rights," among them being "life, liberty, and the pursuit of happiness."

"Illiberal" nations are a more diverse collection, ranging from right wing authoritarian dictatorships to left wing totalitarian regimes. The ideological differences between authoritarian and totalitarian governments are not at all clear and represent an analytical problem that falls outside the scope of this discussion. Instead, here we will focus on liberal systems only and the ideological conservative (right) and radical (left) positions represented within liberal societies.

As was suggested above, the underlying principles of liberalism apply to economic, political, and social issues. *Economic liberalism (free enterprise* to its supporters; *capitalism* to its detractors) is represented by an economy based on private-property rights, free labor, commercial credit, and a relatively open market, where prices and the quality and quantity of commodities presumably fluctuate according to the supply of goods and the public demand for them. *Political liberalism,* or "representative (republican) democracy," is based on universal suffrage—the right of the citizens to elect their political representatives who, in turn, write the laws of government. *Social liberalism,* sometimes called "pluralism" or "egalitarianism," is based on the premise that all citizens are created equal and therefore ought to enjoy the same social rights and opportunities, regardless of race or creed.

Conservatives are called such because they seek to preserve the principles by which liberal societies currently operate. By contrast, radicals seek to fundamentally restructure the system. "Radical" comes from the Latin *radix,* meaning "root." Necessary and acceptable change, say the radicals, will reach beyond surface issues to the roots of the existing system.[3]

Conservatives and radicals debate the relative merits of the dominant institutions of liberal society. For example, given their rather dim view of human nature, economic conservatives argue in favor of "free markets" which—they say—tend to reward those individuals who are most deserving. If, as they say, people are naturally selfish, it is wise to support an economic system which operates on the assumption that people are pri-

---

3. The approach used here is, of course, a "pure type" analysis. Few, if any, people are purely radical or conservative, but it helps us sort things out in our minds if these issues are presented as if they are. Moreover, in the "real world," conservatism and radicalism are far more complex than is presented here. For example, conservatives in the West tend to be "technological radicals," allowing for technological innovations to run their course in a version of the free market system. Such unchecked innovation can have radical impacts on existing institutions (as, for example, the invention of the mass-produced automobile had on the family).

marily motivated to seek their own personal interests. They say that part of capitalism's merit is in the way it operates consistently with human nature; since selfishness ("the pursuit of self-interest") is natural, our economic system ought to be consistent with this tendency. Besides, that way, selfishness will not only be beneficially channeled, but will be contained as well. Failure to recognize the way humans are naturally inclined is the main problem with socialism, they say.

My primary interest in analyzing the various ideological positions within liberal society is to reveal and underscore the values implicit in them (see figure 4). To do so, consider the conservative advocacy of economic liberalism. It is an economic system based on the promise that individual citizens who have the greatest talent, and the desire to put these talents into practice, will be appropriately rewarded. A theory of justice is packed inside these assumptions—one which is associated with the freedom to do with one's property as one pleases (and the promise of sufficient opportunity to do so). This theory, sometimes called "the entitlement theory of justice," declares that justice is best served when, as individuals, citizens are rewarded in proportion to what they have personally earned. The monetary value of their efforts is determined by the marketplace.

Obviously, this theory of justice and its corresponding definitions of freedom and equality is deeply individualistic in nature. In fact, the centrality of individualism is the key value in conservative ideologies predominating in liberal societies.

There is more to the ideological defense of economic liberalism; through hard work and talent, the "more worthy" citizens rise in the social order, justifying their dominance and allowing greater general prosperity throughout society. Thus, the position of the rich is legitimated in two ways: first, they personally deserve their rewards because they earned them; and second, their successes increase the probability that others will share in the system's greater productivity. (The latter justification seems to be far more popular today, given the relatively greater legitimacy accorded to the value of equality.)

Of course, radicals see things quite differently. To them, wealth production is a "zero-sum process," which means that the winners win precisely because the losers lose. For me to become richer, someone else has to become poorer. Radicals therefore

Fig. 4   **Common Characteristics of Conservative and Radical
          Ideologies Within Liberal (i.e., Western) Nations**

Ideological Issues	Radicals ("The Left")	Conservatives ("The Right")
View of human nature:	people are products of their social environments	people are free to choose, and are thus responsible
Tend to focus on:	people as part of large social categories	individuals with unique differences
Definition of existing class system (i.e., capitalism):	bad/oppressive should be replaced	good/necessary should be preserved
Wealth production is:	zero-sum	positive-sum
Main "enlightenment" values: Freedom:	from class oppression	to exercise property rights
Equality:	of social result	of economic opportunity

define wealth creation as inherently exploitative. They believe
that justice cannot be achieved in a capitalistic system and seek
its fundamental restructuring—often under the name of
"economic democracy." Their theory of justice is sometimes
called "the pattern theory," for only insofar as the productive
system is fundamentally altered can wealth be shared fairly
(that is, evenly according to a preset pattern). In this way, justice
can be achieved. The rejection of private property and competition (and the economic exploitation they foster) also means that
governments must either own or regulate the means of production. Thus, radicals tend to favor one form or another of socialism.

   As we have seen, both radicals and conservatives advocate
liberal values of freedom and equality, but they define these
values differently. Although they often use the same words, they
have sharply contrasting—even contradictory—meanings in
mind. Until these definitional differences are adequately understood, ideological debates cannot be properly understood.

For conservatives, *freedom* is defined in terms of the owner's right to choose how private property will be handled. They seek freedom in terms of so-called fair play. For radicals, *freedom* is defined in collective terms—as freedom from class exploitation and oppression. To them, freedom is defined as "fair shares." Conservatives define "equality" in terms of equality of economic opportunity for each individual, whereas radicals define it in terms of equality of economic result.

The major ideological issue in American society is therefore the tension between freedom and equality—both values defined in association with two contrasting models of justice. Most Americans are deeply committed to these values, but we are not ever exactly sure how to define them properly. In our hearts, we are all (small *d*) democrats—that is, radical egalitarians; we warm to the ideal of solidarity amongst equals. In our minds, however, we are conservative libertarians; I want to be free to do with mine what I prefer. You do too. So we seek policies that maximize individual freedoms. The basic ideological tension within liberal nations, then, is between the desire for collective equality and exercise of individual rights.[4]

Our political and economic debates reflect this tension. Consider our USA election contribution laws. Most (small *d*) democrats would object if they thought our government were truly a plutocracy—one in which only the rich have a realistic chance of becoming elected officials. We would (and do) object because such a system ("the best government money can buy") is unequal—and therefore unjust. That is how the majority in the U.S. Congress felt in the mid-1970s after the Watergate scandal;

---

4. There are, of course, many more subtle variations on these themes. For example, the conservative side of the ideological spectrum is not of one mind. There are minority and majority positions among conservatives. The majority (and by far stronger position) is taken by "libertarian conservatives" who advocate the protection of individual rights, and among other things, a corresponding reduction in governmental regulation. This is the type of conservatism considered here.

The minority position is sometimes called "organic conservatism." These conservatives take a much more collectivistic stance, arguing that a strong moral consensus is fundamental to the stability of society. Where the libertarians tend toward individualism and relativity (that is, pluralism) of values, the organicists tend toward collectivism and absolutism.

The differences between these two groups can sometimes be striking. Although some conservative theorists claim that the two positions can be (and, in fact, have been) integrated, many others (myself included) remain unconvinced.

they passed a law stipulating that no citizen could contribute more than one thousand dollars per political campaign. Is this fair? What if campaigns were financed by the candidates' own money? Several years ago, the Supreme Court decided that laws prohibiting private property rights (that is, the spending of one's own money) represent an abridgement of individual freedoms guaranteed by the Constitution. Because of that ruling, now relatively rich candidates can spend all they want of their own money in order to finance their own campaigns, whereas relatively poor candidates have to manage with a maximum one thousand dollars contribution per person per campaign. Is this fair? We can (and do) have many arguments about issues like this—issues that reduce to the tensions between our values concerning individual freedoms and collective equality.

The Tenets of Individualism

Conservatism—generally speaking the most pervasive Western ideology (especially in the USA)—is centered on the value of individualism. Individualism, in turn, is based on several important assumptions, which can be phrased in these ways:

Reductionism. Conservatives claim that society represents the sum of its parts—that is, its citizens. The nation is its citizenry and nothing more. The moral character of the nation is therefore generated by the sum of each individual citizen's character. Conservatives reject the radical assumption that a social system is greater than the sum of its parts: that parts must therefore be understood in terms of properties of the whole. (This is a crucial belief to be examined in greater detail in the next chapter.)

Individual Accountability. Individualists assume that all citizens are (or ought to be) equally responsible for their own social positions. This assumption is usually accompanied by a claim that sufficient opportunity exists (or ought to exist, with a little more reform) within the social order.

Conservatives accept the idea that people rise and fall in the system due to their own personal qualities, and not those of the society itself. The system is benign; it is simply an arena in which individuals compete to determine who is fittest.

Benevolent Self-interest. Individualists believe that as citizens compete to maximize their personal interests (within proper legal limits of course), the welfare of society as a whole is insured. The compatibility of private interests and national welfare is presumably generated by means of "the free market" and by the interplay of competitive interests.

These are the major tenets of individualism, and as such, they promote conservative ideological commitments. Together they promote the view that all liberal institutions (that is, "free enterprise," representative government, religious denominationalism, the adversarial system of law, and so forth) are benign institutions. In other words, social problems like crime, unemployment, and poverty do not spring from the social system itself but from the personal failure of individuals.

If the conservative in question is an orthodox Christian, the source of the problems is likely to be expressed in terms of sin—people are too greedy, lustful, lazy, or whatever. Again, it's not institutional structures (society) that is the source of the problems, but the people themselves.

Individualism tends to deflect potential criticism away from political, economic, and social institutions and on to individual citizens. It is this deflection that accounts for the conservative ideological commitments of individualists. Evangelicals redefine these conservative sentiments in their own spiritualized terms (such as, personal piety, individualistic conceptions of sin, and individual salvation).

For these reasons many conservative Christians equate "conservative" with "orthodox." This equation is, I think, mistaken. One's Christian orthodoxy need not determine one's ideological commitments (nor vice versa). The fact that most orthodox Christians are also ideological conservatives is not an adequate basis to equate the terms. Instead, Christians ought to exercise the capacity to critically appraise all ideological claims, selecting those positions most compatible with Christian ethical principles as well as the circumstances in which they find themselves. (The Christian principle of love, for example, will have to be manifested differently in different cultural settings.) Even more importantly, Christians need the capacity to "think Christianly" even when such thinking places them outside the boundaries set by contemporary ideological debate. I will illustrate this point with respect to economic systems.

An Alternative Christian Economic View

The temptation is always with us to base our understanding of the gospel on our ideological outlooks. For example, conservative Christians typically read their Bibles in the light of middle-class individualism. To accomplish this task, many chapters (for instance, Amos 5; James 2; 1 John 1) have to be either ignored or exegetically twisted beyond recognition. (Similar things can be said about radical Christians.)[5]

Who is to settle the matter, since no one is free from all ideological biases? The orthodox desire is to let the Word of God speak directly, but alas, the Word must be interpreted, and interpretation begs ideological bias to operate.

In terms of economic policy, most evangelicals assume that capitalism is God's way of doing business. An editorial in *Christianity Today* stated the matter pointedly: "Capitalism is biblical."[6] By implication, then, socialism is not.

Yet the tenets of economic individualism—reductionism, individual accountability, and the assumption of benevolent self-interest—are not biblical values, but are instead seventeenth- and eighteenth-century Enlightenment values. These ideas arose and became widespread long after Christianity was established in European society. In fact, the Enlightenment — including the economic ideas giving rise to modern capitalism— can more fairly be seen as part of the disestablishment of Christianity.

---

5. My critical remarks are directed more at conservative evangelicals because they represent, far and away, the majority of contemporary evangelicals.

6. Quoted in Dennis P. Hollinger's *Individualism and Social Ethics*, p. 148. *See also* Harold Lindsell, *Free Enterprise: A Judeo-Christian Defense*. Wheaton: Tyndale, 1982, Franky Schaeffer, ed., *Is Capitalism Christian?* Westchester, IL: Crossway, 1985.

The origins of the Enlightenment were overwhelmingly secular. Increased social pluralism brought on by industrialization (among other structural changes) supported an emerging world view centered on the rights of individual citizens.[7] Potent new ideologies based on liberal ideas both reflected and influenced widespread political, economic, and social changes, most notably in England, the Americas, and France.

Conservative Christians in the USA often associate the founding of the United States with Christian values. For example, they identify the U.S. Constitution as a Christian document—ignoring the fact that most of its signers were outspoken deists; that God is never mentioned (nor even implied) in it; that its major ideas (such as, the legal rights of citizens and the separation of church and state) reflect humanistic and secular values.

Other facile equations are made between Western institutions and Christianity. As I already noted, capitalism is assumed by many conservative Christians to be an outgrowth of Christian values, while socialism is assumed to be its antithesis. Actually, neither capitalism nor socialism are products of Christianity. The philosophers who popularized both systems—Adam Smith and Karl Marx—differed sharply over the legitimacy of private property and the proper role of the state in regulating economic exchange; but they both agreed that economies are fully materialistic systems operating on the basis of what they both defined as "natural law." Moreover, both men argued that economies run on an entirely humanistic basis: capitalism on the basis of supply and demand, and socialism on the basis of governmental regulation. In neither system is divine law and agency given the slightest acknowledgement.

Even so, conservative Christians in capitalistic countries (like the U.S.) often equate capitalism with Christian values, while the opposite tendency exists among Christians in socialist countries (like Zambia). It often seems that Christians are far busier reconciling doctrine to ideological commitment than the other way around.

---

7. True, the Protestant Reformation sponsored its own reactions, but it is usually interpreted as a sixteenth-century preliminary to the Enlightenment.

Christians need to recognize that the gospel is not a matter of natural law. Nor does the gospel center on either individual competition or government regulation. Instead, the primary values of the gospel center on loving relationships within what might be called "organic units" (families, communities, churches). Moreover, the focus is on *spiritual* values, not property rights and productive capacity.

To equate either capitalism or socialism with Christianity is to lose sight of how countercultural (actually, extracultural) the gospel is. We should not seek to fashion a Christian alternative by borrowing the best features of both systems, for both are based on assumptions and values which are incompatible with Christian beliefs and values. Instead, we should start off with Christian values, constructing a truly alternative system which shares none of the foundational values of either capitalism or socialism.

Of course the Bible contains no blueprint for the political economy of God's kingdom. Even so, certain fundamental ethical principles are repeatedly stressed. Our challenge as Christians is to try and read the Bible by first laying aside our ideological presuppositions. Alas, there doesn't seem to be much evidence of this happening. Both radical and conservative Christians seem to be able to find only those biblical references which support their respective ideological conclusions.

The question we are left with is this: can we read the Bible in the way orthodox Christians have always argued it must be read, as God's truth revealed? To the degree we can, it will be our ideological commitments that will be subject to change, not God's truth.

If I wanted to remain objective, in a scholarly sense, I'd simply point out the problem (as I have), give it a sociological explanation, and leave the matter there. But why live like that? Casting better judgment aside, I will attempt to sketch out the parameters of an alternative Christian political economy. If the Bible "speaks," then it ought to give us some guidance on these matters. I believe it does.

It seems to me the Bible generally supports an economic system in which:

1. People come before things. The chief ethical principle of Christianity is not competition, maximal productivity,

GNP, equality of result or of opportunity, private property, or income redistribution. The chief principle involves establishing and maintaining right relationships—"right" as defined by God's law, the chief expression of which is forsaking personal interest for the meeting of each other's needs. This is the heart of *shalom*.

2. Economic value lies in the type of relationships people have with each other—between how people relate together regarding the material object, rather than about the material object itself. The material object is never the end, always the means.

3. The proper economic relationship is one of love—that is, self-sacrificial concern for others, rather than in self-interest, or in some universalized standard of coerced equality maintained by the state.

4. The unit of economic relation is the covenantal group, not the individual or the state. Within a covenantal group, members are joined by a common commitment to Christ and Christ's example. The Bible describes such relations in terms of *koinonia* (which means "sharing intimately in each other's lives," "bearing one another's burdens," and so forth).

General assumptions such as these point toward a community-based political economy.[8] Such an arrangement could not possibly serve as an alternative to a national political economy within an industrialized nation. Accordingly, such an arrangement could only join together Christians within a small voluntary church community. Furthermore, when such Christian communities are formed, they are truly countercultural movements, operating on ethical principles not even recognized by most modern people—ones which would befuddle capitalists and socialists alike.

In such countercultural communities, the quality of human relationships routinely dominate in priority the quantity of

---

8. I am not describing a utopia here. Such cooperative arrangements already exist—in some cases on a significant scale. Relatively large numbers of "worker cooperatives" can be found in Spain, Germany, and the USA. The philosophical bases of such cooperatives vary widely, but none are strictly capitalistic or socialistic. They are clearly reflective of a third way.

goods produced. Ownership of the means of production is spread throughout the work force, so that relationships are maintained on an integrated and consensual basis. Each worker owns shares in the means of production. Property and control are not in the hands of the state or corporate managers. All sorts of mischief is created when people who neither own nor manage property work for those who do, or when distant and self-serving bureaucrats dictate who will work where, for how much, and under what conditions.

Nevertheless, under an alternative Christian economy, outer limits must be set by the worker-owners as to how much and how little people can own and earn, assuming some sort of personal accountability for productivity is maintained. Under such a system, a state-imposed universal egalitarianism is avoided, but so is a competitive free-for-all. Neither the politically powerful nor the economically wealthy is left free to dominate the powerless and the poor.

This discussion has to be cut short; my purpose here is not to map out a fully operational Christian economic order, but only to illustrate that Christian ethical principles can be used to stimulate our thinking in ways not even hinted at in the *cosmos*.

In the New Testament the followers of Christ are repeatedly called to come out and be separated from the *cosmos*. Separation ought to begin with the capacity to think away the conventional ideological arguments which may or may not be compatible with Christian values—a renewing of our minds, as it were. It is unbecoming (to say the least) for orthodox Christians to continue to think only within the parameters of conventional reality and to bestow legitimacy on whatever humanistic economic system is currently dominant.[9]

We therefore come full circle to the need for ideological awareness: critical reassessment begins with an adequate understanding of ideological influences.

---

9. Actually, the tendency to equate existing institutions like capitalism and representative democracy with Christian principles is more a function of conventionality than conservatism. As such, our analysis as to why Christians tend to be conservatives needs to include the discussion of localism and parochialism given in chapter 2. Even though many conservatives are also deeply conventional (that is, uncritically accepting of the existing society), the two impulses are somewhat separate and deserve to be analyzed as such.

A Look Ahead

The fact remains that orthodox Christians are overwhelmingly conservative. The key to their ideological conservatism is their commitment to an individualistic view of things. However, before we turn to the individualism of evangelical Christians in chapter 7, we need to inquire into a preliminary matter.

Keep in mind that our overall purpose is to understand the relationship between sociology and Christianity. Implicit within each perspective are certain values and analytical styles that have definite ideological implications. In the next chapter, we shall examine two different questions about why people tend to think and act as they do. We will discover that the questions we ask about social reality are often prompted by implicit ideological assumptions often taken for granted—assumptions that, for conservative Christians, relate to the values of individualism just reviewed. We need to understand fully the nature of questions typically asked by sociologists and how they compare to the questions asked by most conservative Christians who are not yet familiar with the discipline.

6

Two Very Different Questions

Friday the 13th, March, 1964, was a bad day for Catherine "Kitty" Genovese. It was also her last. On her way back from her late-night job, she was brutally attacked just outside her New York City apartment. For about thirty horrifying minutes, starting around 3:00 A.M., Miss Genovese was repeatedly beaten and stabbed, finally fatally. During the attacks she screamed, fought off her assailant, and tried to escape, but to no avail. Kitty Genovese died before the police finally arrived on the scene. The following day a brief article about the murder was tucked away on page 22 of the *New York Times*. Another murder in a city known for its violence.

However, information would soon emerge which indicated this murder was unusual. During the following week, the police discovered that no fewer than thirty-eight of Kitty's neighbors knew about the assault while it was happening. Even so, not one of them bothered to call the police until it was too late.

By the next Saturday, this new information propelled the story onto the front pages of most American newspapers.

I was a college student home on spring vacation when the Genovese murder became a national story. As I sat in church the next day, I was not surprised to learn that the pastor had also heard the terrible news. Instead of his prepared sermon, we heard an analysis of the crime and what it signified. The same impromptu analysis was given in churches all over the country, as Americans tried to comprehend what kind of nation we had become. A woman had been brutally attacked and murdered. Thirty-eight of her neighbors knew what was going on. Not one of them tried to help her.

No one had any doubts about the evil character of Kitty Genovese's assailant. But what of the thirty-eight neighbors? They were described by our minister as "cold," "uncaring," "merciless," "heartless"—in a word, apathetic. Were these people prototypes of the modern American? Were *we* like these people?

Whatever the answer to these questions, our pastor knew the reason why no one had responded to Miss Genovese's screams for help: *sin*. Terrible events such as this one demonstrate all too clearly the depths to which our sinful natures can carry us.

While I did not doubt then (nor do I doubt now) that humans are sinful, the pastor's explanation did not strike me as satisfactory. The reason for my dissatisfaction was simple; I had learned in a philosophy course a relatively simple idea: that a constant cannot adequately explain a variable. It was clear that Kitty Genovese's murder could not be accounted for with reference to a condition that applies equally to all people. After all, *I* had not murdered anyone, yet I was a sinner just like the murderer.

I knew something important was missing from the minister's explanation. It was not until I started my career as a sociologist, however, that I was able to discover a more satisfactory analysis.[1]

The Sociological Perspective

The crucial question involved in sociological analyses can be underscored by means of a classical social-psychological experiment conducted by Bibb Latane and Judy Rodin in 1969, several years after the infamous murder. Their experiment centered on what had by then become known as "bystander apathy."

---

1. In particular, it wasn't until I read the excellent account of "bystander apathy" in Elliot Aronson's *The Social Animal*.

In their experiment, students were asked to fill out a questionnaire given to them by a woman assistant. After starting the students on the questionnaire, and informing them that she would return in a while, she went into an adjoining room. Soon the students heard the sounds of someone stepping up on a chair, the sound of the chair splintering and a body crashing to the floor, followed by a woman's anguished moans ("My foot . . . I think it's broken . . ."). The students had every reason to believe the woman in the next room had been seriously injured. (Actually, what they heard was a tape recording, but they could not know this unless they entered the room.)

The purpose of the experiment was to explore, first of all, the conditions under which people would help each other, and second, to find out what percentage of the students would remain passive, and what percentage would act like good Samaritans. For obvious reasons, this experiment became known as "the lady in distress" experiment.

The situation contrived by the researchers was somewhat similar to what happened in the Genovese case. In both instances, a woman was hurt, and others knew about it, and in both situations considerable bystander apathy apparently resulted. Of course, given the proximity of the bystanders to the "victim" (and considering the fact that the latter situation did not take place at 3:00 A.M.), we would expect a much higher rate of intervention, which turned out to be the case.

However, there is an additional interesting facet to the experimental situation. Latane and Rodin compared two experimental situations—the first in which there was only one student bystander, and a second, in which there were two. They conducted many separate trials of each experimental situation. When a single student was seated in the room, the response rate was about 70 percent. In other words, in seven out of every ten experimental trials, the student seated alone quickly responded to the pleas for help. But when two students were together in the room, in only about 40 percent of the trials did one or more of the students intervene. That's a significant drop of 30 percent.

Note that there are two features of this situation that deserve careful analysis. On the one hand, we want to know why some students responded quickly to the cries for help, while others remained in their seats, apparently apathetic. This sort of differential response occurred in all the experimental situations, regardless of how many persons were in the room. Whether there were one or two students in the room, certain students rushed in to offer help, while others remained in their seats. An obvious question arises: what kind of people would just sit there when, in the very next room, an injured person calls out for help? What sort of personal traits separate those who respond from those who do not?

Most people would ask this type of question upon hearing about the experiment. I certainly did.

However, there is another type of question which could be asked, although I suspect it would occur to fewer people. In addition to wanting to know why some people did and other people did not offer assistance, we could also want to know why there was such a significant difference in the percentage of good Samaritans in one situation (when only one person was in the room) compared to the other (when there were two). Why the 30 percent drop?

Thus we have two important questions here. The first inquires into the matter of individual character differences. In sharp contrast, the second is a question about situational differences involving group rates of action.

Since these are two very different types of questions, we must distinguish between them if we are going to make any analytical headway at all. The number of people in a room is not in any conceivable way reducible to matters of individual traits— moral or otherwise. When it comes to questions involving differential rates of behavior, inquiry into personal character is completely beside the point.[2] Likewise, no amount of information about social structure can tell us why one person responds one way while another person *in the same situation* acts differently. Thus, we have two distinct lines of inquiry in analyzing any social situation.

A Question of Structure

Remember that the presence or absence of another student was the only structural feature distinguishing the two experi-

---

2. Could an overrepresentation of good Samaritans somehow manage to show up in one but not the other type of experimental situation? Since Latane and Rodin randomly assigned their students to the experimental situations, this alternative explanation is, to say the least, not likely.

mental situations. Using so-called common sense (which in American culture tends to focus on individual differences), we would suppose that the presence of more people would increase the probability of intervention, since the more people, the greater the probability that at least one good Samaritan would be present. The more people, the greater the odds, right? Well, as in so many cases, common sense is misleading. Remember, when the number of bystanders increased, the tendency to intervene actually *decreased*.

Let's see how sociologists would go about analyzing these results. As we have seen, sociologists begin their analyses with a relatively simple idea: social reality is not an inherent property of the situation but is instead a property conferred upon the situation by the actors present. In other words, "reality" is what the people involved define it to be.

Once we have this idea in mind, we realize that so-called emergencies do not come predefined. Until the situation is defined as "an emergency," it is not an emergency at all. True, someone may be injured, perhaps even killed. This much is objective and occurs no matter how the situation is defined. Even so, whatever objectively occurs is not an emergency unless and until it is defined as such by the participants.

We begin our sociological analysis of differential response rates by applying the simple idea just discussed: when two students are seated in the room together, each one will define "reality" by means of a simple procedure—that is, by noting available cues in the situation (such as, the sounds coming from the next room, the action of other students, and so forth), as well as by recalling similar situations and the meanings associated with them.

Of course, for the student who is seated alone, there is no action to observe. In this case, the situation must be defined exclusively on the basis of previously learned definitions and auditory cues coming from the next room. Remember that this combination of factors produced an intervention rate of about 70 percent. In the other situation, however, where each student had another student's action to observe, the rate dropped to 40 percent. Why?

Let's consider the situation as though you were one of the two students. First, you hear strange sounds coming from the next room. What is going on in there? Like most people in an ambiguous situation, you first glance out of the corner of your eye at the other student. Of course, the other student is in the same state of indecision. Consequently, you both observe the same thing: a student sitting there working on the assignment. What do you make of that?

Assuming you are a fairly typical person, you probably carry in your mind the following taken-for-granted maxim: "Whenever there is an emergency, people get up and do something about it." Well, is this "an emergency" or not? Apparently not: after all, the other person is just sitting there. Therefore, you stay put. But note the irony of the situation: the other person is going through the same thought process you are! So, you both sit there while the moans slowly subside in the next room.

When seen in this way, what we have here is not so much a matter of "moral failure" or "bystander apathy," but of simple conformity to group norms. Whatever the condition of your personal morality, the structure of action has influenced the plausibility of defining the situation as a "nonemergency." To explain what is going on, we need to look to the structure of the social situation—a situation which in no way is reducible to the moral character of each participant.

A Question of Character

Remember, there are two analytical questions we could ask. The first question is "Why are the *rates* of intervention so different between the two situations?" The explanation already given seems adequate. (Of course, it needs to be subjected to further empirical testing.) The principal cause here appears to be the organization of action in the situation—in this case, the simple matter of the number of individuals in the room. When another student is introduced into the situation, the rate of helping drops significantly.

However, a second (entirely different) question can be asked. We need to inquire also about why each particular student did or did not become involved. In both situations, some students did and others did not respond to the moans coming from the next room. Apparently, regardless of who else was in the room, some students said to themselves, "*You* can sit there and do nothing if you want to, but *I* am going to find out what happened." Why the difference?

Whereas the first question—the one inquiring into differential group rates—has nothing to do with moral character, this second question could have everything to do with it. For such problems, inquiry into individual differences, including differences in moral character, is a perfectly valid approach. Perhaps some people are generally more helpful than others—regardless of structural circumstances.

Whether the cause of the intervention results from differences in moral character, personality, or (for all I know) genetic inheritance, is not our concern here. The important point is that the explanation, whatever its particular focus, will involve inquiry into individual differences.

Thus, we have at least two distinct types of questions to ask when we seek to explain what is happening socially. Whereas the approach taken to answer the first question (about group rates) is structural and deterministic, the approach to the second question (about individual differences) is quite different. Here it is possible that individual choice is a crucial factor whereas in accounting for differences in group rates it is irrelevant.

Analytical Perspective and Ideology

We need to understand clearly that there are subtle and infrequently recognized connections between the ideological assumptions (discussed in the last chapter) and the types of questions typically asked about social reality explored in this chapter. Remember that individualism is one of the chief value commitments of conservatives—a value commitment connected to an analytical perspective in which questions about structural issues are typically denied or ignored. Conservatives are more likely to ask questions which focus on the nature of individual differences. Radicals, on the other hand, are more likely to inquire into the structures of social action.

Both radicals and conservatives tend to be "analytically imperialistic." They tend to answer both types of questions—about individual differences and group rates—with the same type of analysis. While this is a serious mistake, it is also a common one. To impose a structural form of analysis on both sets of questions (as many sociologists do) pushes questions of individual character and free will to the background. On the other hand, to impose an individualistic analysis (as many conservative Christians do) ignores vital questions pertaining to institutional forces which shape our action and consciousness.

The significance of this connection between ideology and analytical approach will, I hope, be much clearer after our discussion in the next chapter. There we will seek to answer the question why conservative Christians are often threatened by sociology.

7

Why Sociology Threatens Christians

Christians often react with surprise as well as fascination to their first encounter with sociology. Many also react as if the sociological way of looking represents a distinct threat—an unwelcomed challenge to secure and firmly established habits of thoughts. I have long been intrigued by this rather defensive response and have often reflected on the possible connections between the perceived threat sociology poses and the Christian commitments of my students.

Of course, some of the shock has little or nothing to do with the students' Christianity. Some of it can be attributed to their relative inexperience with liberal education. They are usually not prepared for the systematic, abstract, analytical approach required and generated by such studies. In this respect, sociology is just one more shock among many for students inadequately prepared for the complexities they encounter in college.[1]

---

1. Of course, there are other factors, such as the demeanor of the professor, to take into consideration. However, here I will concentrate on those factors which are common to all sociology courses, rather than those which distinguish one course from another.

Additional shock comes from the sort of outlook sociology espouses simply because it has adopted a scientific (that is, a skeptical) perspective. Scientific skepticism is directed against "common knowledge"—of the sort the student has always relied upon. It is even directed at perception itself, starting with the assumption that all humans are biased.

However, it is not merely scientific skepticism that bothers these students. It is more a matter of what sorts of concerns the skepticism is directed toward. Sociology's skepticism is directed toward the social world, which to many students is more unsettling than skepticism directed toward the natural world. Because we have been raised in a culture that generally accepts the legitimacy of technological change and the scientific way of looking at nature, we can usually take in stride ideas which are far from obvious—for instance, that time is not a constant or that light from stars takes centuries to reach us. Besides, Christian college students generally regard the discoveries of natural science as the revelation of God's creative acts. This assumption goes a long way toward legitimizing whatever shocks may come from their scientific studies.

There's usually a different reaction, however, when scientific skepticism is directed at society. Most of us can accept the idea that the natural world is more complex than it appears to be more readily than we can when the same idea is directed at social reality. It is one thing to be told that the sun isn't actually where we see it now. It is quite another thing to be told that our sense of social reality is just one of many equally viable ways of seeing, and that institutional arrangements we often take for granted are relative and arbitrary human constructions.

There is at least one additional reason why many Christian students find the messages of sociology particularly hard to take (more so, I think, than non-Christian students). Sociological research reveals that orthodox Christians tend to be more socially conservative and thus more committed to traditional ways of acting and thinking than are Christians who are less doctrinally orthodox (Wuthnow, 1973). Such students also tend to be more culturally parochial—perhaps more naive than their non-Christian peers—and thus more threatened by a mode of analysis which mounts a full-scale attack on parochialism.

Furthermore, one would expect that the degree of threat generated by sociological relativity would be directly proportional to the tendency of a person to define social reality in absolute terms. Conservative Christians struggle with suggestions that the nuclear family is merely one of many functional alternatives, or that our system of criminal justice is biased against the poor and that it may be considerably less just than we prefer to think.

Dealing with these and other routine sociological insights is troublesome enough—especially for those evangelical students raised in ideologically conservative homes (as most are). But when sociological relativity is focused on *religion,* as it inevitably is, the threat can become acute. Christianity—nothing more than a human invention? Anyone who takes religion and religious truth seriously will not sit still, unmoved, in the face of this type of challenge.

I have already dealt with the difficult issue of relativity and religious truth in chapter 4. Here we deal with another source of tension between these two perspectives—the issue of ideological definitions of individual freedom and structural determinism.

The Sociological Imagination

We begin with one of the most quoted paragraphs in sociological literature:

> Nowadays men often feel that their private lives are a series of traps. They sense that within their everyday worlds, they cannot overcome their troubles, and in this feeling, they are often quite correct; what ordinary men are directly aware of and what they try to do are bounded by the private orbits in which they live; their visions and their powers are limited to the closeup scenes of job, family, neighborhood; in other milieux, they move vicariously and remain spectators. And the more aware they become, however vaguely, of ambitions and of threats which transcend their immediate locales, the more trapped they seem to feel (Mills, 1959, p. 3).

This is the opening paragraph from a book by C. Wright Mills entitled *The Sociological Imagination.* His observation that the world is becoming more complex and as a result, more confusing and problematic, is as commonplace as it is accurate. Mills offered the sociological imagination as a way of realistically comprehending the problems of living in our complex modern world. Since we are unlikely to solve problems we do not first correctly understand, the sociological imagination has an immediate and practical purpose. Mills intended that educated citizens could use this special way of looking at the world to understand, cope with, and perhaps alter their social environments.[2]

Many citizens correctly perceive the world as fraught with problems arising from vast impersonal social forces beyond their capacity to control—and even to fully comprehend. The recognition of these threatening social forces often results in feelings of helplessness, alienation, and eventual apathy. Many people respond by retreating into their own private lives where there is still some sense of personal control. After all, if parents cannot control the increasing rate of familial instability, at least they can control their own children's dating habits. Sadly, this sense of control is often illusionary; the dating habits of one's children are inescapably linked to a wider system of action over which one has little control—and about as much comprehension.

One of Mills' most important contributions was the distinction between "personal troubles" and "social issues." Both terms refer to conditions commonly defined as "problems."

Troubles are personal problems arising out of the peculiar traits of individuals, as well as from personal relationships with other people. Reasonably enough, the appropriate solution to a personal trouble is found at the individual level. For example, if a person is unemployed because of personal laziness, lack of appropriate skills, or because of a failure to get along with others, then the problem is correctly addressed as a personal trouble. Its appropriate solution will also be individualistic in nature (that is, the person somehow has to be motivated, retrained, or given a "personality adjustment").

---

2. In this respect, Mills was an outspoken advocate of value-directed sociology. As such, he did not advocate scientific knowledge for its own sake. Instead, the tools of social science were to be applied to problems defined by his explicit, ideologically radical values in order to promote humanitarian, socialistic, and democratic goals.

However, a social *issue* is a different matter. Issues grow out of institutional arrangements and as such, refer to how the social system is structured. For example, when the economy declines, thousands of people are thrown out of work—not necessarily because each person is lazy, insufficiently skilled, or maladjusted, but because the structure of economic opportunity has collapsed. As a result, no amount of changes in personal motivation or training will be sufficient to solve issues like structural unemployment. True, each unemployed person could try to work harder, obtain new skills, or try to get along better, but when there are not enough jobs, the basic issue—unemployment—will not (indeed, *cannot*) go away.

Of course, Mills realized that any given problem—like unemployment—may be caused by a combination of forces, some of them related to the personal characteristics of the unemployed person, while others may have nothing to do with particular people at all. Even so, Mills emphasized the differences between troubles and issues in order to make his point as clearly as possible and to emphasize that the correct analysis of one is not necessarily appropriate for the other.[3]

Reductionism and Emergentism

The tendency to reduce issues to troubles—to ignore or be ignorant of the structural sources of problems—is an analytical style sometimes called "reductionism."[4] This analytical style stands in sharp contrast to the analytical style preferred by most sociologists—"emergentism." While not all sociologists are equally emergentistic, they agree that societies represent complex social systems and that the parts cannot be properly understood in isolation from the whole.

---

3. I took this same approach in chapter 5, writing as if conservative and radical ideologies could be sharply dichotomized when, in fact, they are subtly and complexly interrelated. As Mills recognized, creating conceptual dichotomies is often a necessary first step in our analysis. After making these unrealistic "pure-type" dichotomous distinctions, I will attempt to show how other complexities can enter into the analysis.

4. The word *reductionism* has a number of definitions. The one I am using here is not the standard one. More commonly, "reductionism" refers to the tendency of positivistically inclined scientists to reduce all nonempirical (including supernatural) phenomena to natural phenomena. Included also is the effort to understand systems by reducing them to their constituent parts. This second usage (sometimes called "elementalism" or "atomism") is the one used here.

Images of what societies are really like sharply differ for reductionists and emergentists. For reductionists, society is like a pile of sand. The pile is itself significant—each grain contributing to its overall shape—but the grains are otherwise independent of each other. The pile is nothing more than all the grains of sand making it up.

For emergentists, the imagery is quite different. Emergentists look at society as a system of interrelated parts—like a machine, or something natural like an organism. When seen as a system, society becomes something more than just the sum of its parts. It is a whole greater than the sum of its parts—a system emerging out of the interaction of its parts.

In addition, images of what society *is* give rise to images of what society *must be.* Correspondingly, what must be leads to an understanding of how we ought to act. In other words, from the metaphysical assumptions about what society must be like comes an ethical perspective about how we ought to act, and what social policies will work best. In short, ideology emerges from metaphysics.

Reality Through Reductionistic Eyes

Middle-class Americans—given their individualistic values—have a preference for seeing things in a reductionistic way.

It is crucial, Mills insisted, to recognize whether a given problem is primarily individualistic or structural in nature. If individualistic solutions are applied to problems that are actually social issues, not only will they fail to correct the problem, they might actually make matters worse.

Middle-class Americans seem to have a special knack for applying individual solutions to what are societal issues, thereby making the problems worse. Since one of our dominant cultural values is individualism, most of us (particularly conservatives) "instinctively" reduce institutional problems to individualistic terms, and thus treat issues as if they were individual troubles only.

Consider the problem of urban crime. When people are mugged, they don't need a sociologist to tell them they have a problem. If the victims are sufficiently wealthy, they solve their problem by moving out of the city to a suburban district, where the crime rate is lower. Whether or not they have defined mugging as an issue or as a trouble, they respond to it as if it *is* a trouble. From their safer suburban havens, they now commute to their jobs in the city. Since 1950, millions of affluent Americans have done exactly this. However, when people solve their individual troubles in this way, they unwittingly contribute to a structural problem; among other results, they help to undermine the social and fiscal stability of the city.

First of all, people who move to the suburbs take their potential tax revenues with them. Since it generally costs more per capita to run a city than a suburb, these resources are a significant loss to the city. There are also other, more subtle, resources lost to the city in this exodus. The people who leave (most likely working- and middle-class people) take their class-specific values and lifestyles with them. Generally speaking, these are the folks who work hard, delay gratification through investments of all kinds, join groups for civic betterment, own their own homes, pay their bills, and so forth. No city can afford to lose its most politically and socially active citizens.

The *trouble* of urban crime is, therefore, overcome (for some) but it is not solved. True, many suburbanites no longer get mugged every time they take a walk. However, as a result of their personal efforts, the *issue* of urban crime usually gets worse. Even if we had rationally planned to generate more crime, we could not have done a better job of it.

Of course, no one collectively planned anything of the sort; all these suburbanites were trying to do is make the best decision in light of the troubles besetting them. Yet, in so doing, the quality of social life declines—including increased crime rates (to say nothing of increased highway congestion, automotive pollution, energy depletion). Their best efforts create situations which frustrate their own desires. As a result, just as Mills predicted, they feel more and more entrapped, despite their considerable efforts to the contrary.

It would be both unfair and incorrect to charge these people with personally plotting the city's economic decline or trying to increase the rate of crime. They don't want to do anything of the sort. All they want to do is get themselves into a safer social environment. Yet, we are not like grains of sand, each independent of all others. Instead, each of us is part of a larger system, and as such, our lives cannot be understood apart from the system, any more than the system can be properly understood apart from our lives. Without a sociological imagination, which links biography to history, our efforts to understand properly who we are—that is, why we act and think as we do—are substantially handicapped. We may think we are solving our problems, and in some respects perhaps we are. But our efforts may also make the problem worse in other respects.

The John Wayne Perspective

A reductionistic (or "troubles-only") perspective rests on the assumption that social problems can be properly understood in terms of personal qualities: moral character, personality, talents, personal choices, and so forth. This view represents what might be called a "John Wayne perspective"—that is, the tendency to analytically associate good or bad situations in terms of good or bad personal qualities. Issues are reduced to troubles; bad societies are the result of too many bad individuals.

Consider the typical western-movie plot. A town is faced with a terrible situation: the town's bank is robbed; its people terrorized; its cattle rustled. Why are all these bad things happening? Why, bad guys, of course. And the obvious solution: get some good guys to get rid of the bad guys (say, John Wayne, or in more modern scenarios, Clint Eastwood, Sylvester Stallone, and so on). The conclusion: bad situations get better when the good guys drive out the bad guys. In each case, the key analytical component of the John Wayne perspective is the moral traits of people. The number of individuals is not usually important; we could be speaking of one person or millions of people.

Reductionistic analyses are encountered quite frequently. Consider, for example, the problem of intergroup conflict. For much of our history, relations between the dominant white majority and certain ethnic and racial minority groups (such as black Americans) have been fraught with conflict. But what exactly is the source of the problem? Reductionistic analyses offered by many psychologists and educators stress the role of prejudice—a negative attitude based on stereotyped images. Many Americans prefer to think that if the prejudiced people would somehow stop being prejudiced, then (and only then) race relations in the USA would cease being such a problem.

When I was a graduate student, the Dean of the School of Education declared a full-scale effort to rid the university of racism. As part of this effort, "sensitivity groups" were established where, among other things, black and white students could get to know each other better. It was thought that people who know each other would understand each other more, and that the improved personal relationships would lessen interracial conflicts. Hence racism would be ended on campus. That seemed pretty convincing to most people.

It wasn't convincing to the professors I studied with in the sociology department, however. They were considerably less optimistic that patterns of race relations could be meaningfully altered simply by getting more blacks and whites to know each other better. True to their sociological imaginations, these sociologists emphasized that a pervasive and complicated system of institutionalized (that is, structural) discrimination exists, and that intergroup relations would continue to be a function of these structures despite how well people got to know each other. In effect, they insisted that structures of inequality cannot be meaningfully reduced to the attitudes individuals have about each other. Changing attitudes without changing the structures which give them rise is like putting bandages on a stroke victim. Such care might give the helpers some satisfaction that they are actively involved, but it won't do anything to alleviate the underlying problem.

The emphasis in my graduate sociology classes centered on institutional patterns of unequal distribution of wealth, political power, and prestige, and how these structures of inequality tend to persist over generations. My professors emphasized that disadvantaged blacks would remain disadvantaged, whether or not they made friends with white people. In short, attitudes may be important, but they are not primary.

The troubles-only focus (in this case, on prejudice as an individual attitude) misses the institutional sources of the problem. In a sense, prejudice is more the effect than the cause of social disadvantages. Prejudice is a symptom of a structural issue. It is the result of a stratification system which routinely results in discrimination on the basis of racial and ethnic identity. True, there probably are certain "inner predispositions" that make some majority group members more bigoted than others. Even so, prejudice is a norm, and as such it is a property of groups—not just a psychological state.

Seen from the issues-perspective of the sociologist, prejudice is a factor in the struggle for group domination. In particular, prejudice is an ideological weapon used by the dominant group. To legitimate their privileged position, members of the dominant group express hostility against minority-group members. In this way, they can assure themselves that minority-group members generally deserve what they get. "Inferior people" deserve to be on the short end of the stick.

The root of the problem, as sociologists look at it, is the inequality structured right into the social system, and not merely the irrational attitudes of certain people. Efforts to eliminate prejudicial attitudes, while alleviating a certain amount of anxiety for some liberally minded people ("at least we're doing something about the problem"), fails to address the ongoing structures of inequality. As such, their liberal programs unintentionally work toward conservative ends—that is, the structure (and the source of on-going prejudice) is perpetuated.

If, in true John Wayne fashion, we spend all our time getting rid of bad guys (such as, reeducating bigots, or getting to know each other better), we will discover to our dismay that our problems will persist. We will also meet few minority group members grateful to us for our humanitarian efforts on their behalf. As a result, we are likely to become frustrated and perhaps a bit angry because the intergroup tensions won't go away. Eventually we may wish that "they" would just go solve "their" problems.

In the movies, John Wayne shoots, jails, or drives out of town all the bad guys and the troubles stop. Social issues aren't like that.

Individualism and Conservatism

I need to stress again what I have already pointed out in chapter 5—that is, the crucial significance of individualism as a key American cultural value. Our commitment to individualism permeates our way of life. Most Americans believe, for example, that poor people are poor at least in part because they have somehow brought their disadvantaged situation on themselves. *It's their own fault.*

The on-going political debate over social welfare in the United States—the debate between conservative Republicans and liberal Democrats—is sustained despite the commitment of both sides to an individualistic way of interpreting poverty. Most members of both parties are convinced that the cause of economic disadvantage lies, in one way or another, with disadvantaged people themselves. Right-wing conservatives usually argue that poor people are somehow personally unfit (that is, they have lousy morals, they don't work hard enough, they don't "delay gratification," they are genetically inferior, or whatever). Let the free market sort them into fit and unfit categories and distribute them accordingly. As conservatives are fond of saying, "The cream always rises to the top."

By contrast, Americans who take a politically liberal approach are more likely to argue that the poor are "culturally disadvantaged." This usually means that liberals think the solution to poverty lies in some sort of therapeutic approach (administered, of course, by a host of government agencies) all intending to cure the poor of their problem.

Although the solutions espoused by both the conservatives and the liberals are strikingly different, the underlying ideological perspective is largely the same: disadvantaged people bring problems on themselves because social problems arise from within. In short, the dominant American political tradition, of whatever ideological commitment, is to "blame the victims" for their victimization (Ryan, 1976). Whether conservative or liberal, most Americans are individualists—and hence reductionists. In this sense, whether they regard themselves as conservatives, moderates, or liberals, Americans share an overriding ideological conservatism based on the value of individualism.

Only the radicals, a tiny fraction of adult Americans, argue that it is American society itself—the institutions of private property, criminal justice, education, and so forth—that cause some people to be poor (and to stay poor), with only rare instances of escape through social mobility.[5] The way to end pov-

---

5. When sociologists argue this way, very few Americans agree, which helps to

erty, they say, is not to "morally convert," educate, or assist the poor as individuals, but to change the system that made them poor in the first place, and keeps them poor.

The emphasis on individual freedom in the form of legal rights for the individual is the hallmark of ideological conservatism within Western democracies. And the point of the discussion thus far is that *the emphasis sociologists place on social issues and the attribution of cause to social structures flies in the face of conservative (that is, individualistic) commitments and reductionistic sensibilities.*

It is this tension, then, that gives rise to the threat perceived by most evangelical students. These students have been, for the most part, raised in ideologically conservative surroundings. As a result, their commitment to individualism is strong. Moreover, their individualism grows out of their pietistic faith. Pietism casts one's eyes inward—to matters of "the heart"—and away from structural issues. Although evangelicals have put considerable distance between themselves and fundamentalists, they share the same metaphysical assumptions that characterize fundamentalism. Such a metaphysic has historically served conservative ideological purposes by dichotomizing the world into *spiritual* and *secular* realms, focusing attention on the spiritual and seeking to separate from the secular. By making sin a personal matter—stressing the evils of fornication, smoking, dancing, swearing, and such (all private acts)—conservative Christians have directed attention inward and hence away from social structural concerns (like the institutionalized sources of poverty).

Fundamentalism arose and is still strongest in the South. It developed in reaction to theological liberalism at a time when white supremacy was strongest in the early part of this century. The point is that the kind of racist regime most whites supported was dubious at best when scrutinized by Christian ethical principles. Such scrutiny could be avoided, however, since funda-

---

demonstrate how pervasive the conservative ideological perspective is within American culture. For example, in 1981, only 6 percent of a national sample of adults thought that poverty causes crime. (Reference: U.S. Department of Justice, Bureau of Justice Statistics, *Sourcebook of Criminal Statistics, 1981,* ed. Timothy J. Flanagan, David J. van Alstyne, and Michael R. Gottfredson [Washington, D.C.: U.S. Government Printing Office], 1982, p. 192.)

mentalism's orientation was deeply individualistic. Consequently, fundamentalists focused on prohibitions against smoking, drinking, sexual promiscuity, and so forth, and avoided matters of political power and economic oppression—matters they regarded as secular and thus irrelevant to the proper exercise of Christian faith.

These pietistic tendencies have persisted into contemporary evangelicalism. Thus, the main theme of sociology—the sociological imagination and its issues-orientation—is upsetting to these troubles-oriented Christians. They have lived and breathed a troubles perspective since early childhood, and the introduction of the sociological perspective—with all its emphasis on structural issues—is somewhat like a bucket of cold water in the face.[6]

More Questions to Resolve

We are left, then, with several questions. First, is ideological conservatism an inherent part of Christianity, or does it represent, in itself, a cultural adaptation that many Christians bring to it? In other words, can we make a legitimate distinction between conservative Christianity, on the one hand, and orthodox Christianity on the other? Second, is sociology inherently ideologically radical—based exclusively on a structural analytical foundation—or is this commitment tacked on to sociology by sociologists who were predisposed toward a radical ideological stance in the first place? In other words, does looking at the world sociologically mean that one must give up attachments to an individualistic moral perspective?

I will argue in the next chapter that both ideological messages—the radicalism of sociology and the conservatism of

---

6. When I talk about "conservative Christians," I am doing so only with respect to their individualistically oriented commitments. Whether this commitment is linked with social, political, or economic conservatism is an open question. It would be a mistake, for example, to assume that most evangelicals are conservative Republicans; they aren't. (Compare with James Hunter's *American Evangelicalism*.)

For an examination of the left-of-center ideological commitments of contemporary sociologists see Everett C. Ladd, Jr., and Seymour M. Lipset, "The 1977 Survey of the American Professoriate," in *Public Opinion,* May/June, 1978, pp. 30–39.

Christianity—have, to some degree, been tacked on. As a result, much of the tension between them, giving rise to the threat many Christians experience when they first encounter sociology, is synthetic and unnecessary.

8

Ideological Assumptions Within Christianity and Sociology

Before moving on to the concerns of this chapter, let's review the argument to this point and indicate where it is going from here. Part 2 began by asking why Christians often feel threatened by sociology. I responded in chapter 5 by observing that orthodox Christians are typically conservative in their ideological orientations. Conservatives tend to be analytically reductionistic—that is, they analyze social reality generally, if not exclusively, in terms of individual differences. In other words, they tend to analyze social problems as if they were what C. Wright Mills called "personal troubles." For example, they tend to explain poverty or crime in terms of individual failures (such as, personal immorality, learning disabilities, or whatever). Structural factors (that is, the institutional patterns by which social action is guided) are typically either ignored or denied.

As discussed in chapter 6, sociologists start with the willingness and ability to define and analyze social reality in terms of institutional arrangements (cultural patterns, roles, and norms) that transcend and direct the behavior and thought of particular people. It is the emphasis on these structures and the ideological implications of this approach that bothers conservatives. These implications contradict (or at least seem to contradict) their own individualistic commitments, with all the emphasis they give to individual moral responsibility and rights. Therefore, many Christians are threatened by sociology primarily because they are *conservatives,* not because they are Christians.

The conservative's individual-as-central sensibility is an orientation that handicaps a more complete understanding of social problems (Lewis, 1978). A troubles-only orientation serves as a set of analytical blinders, sorting out the so-called sensible questions to be asked, and choosing only those explanations which conform to the individual-as-central formula:

"Why are some people poor?"
"Because they want to be poor [or otherwise deserve to be poor]."

"Why didn't Miss Genovese's neighbors help her?"
"Because they are cold, heartless, uncaring people."

"Why is there so much crime?"
"Because there are so many criminally inclined people around."

Now, I certainly think that the moral character of people who rob, rape, and kill leaves a good deal to be desired. I also think that people who engage in these crimes ought to be dealt with severely. However, any analytical approach that focuses exclusively on good guys and bad guys ignores crucial questions. For example, we need to ask why poor people are overrepresented in our prisons. Why are poor people more likely to be arrested, booked, prosecuted, denied bail, found guilty, sent to prison (and sent there for longer periods of time) than are higher-income persons who also commit illegal acts? What about the self-serving and often-dangerous acts of business executives, who typically escape prison either because their activities are not defined as illegal in the first place, or who escape prosecution by a criminal-justice system biased in their favor

(Reiman, 1984)? These are not questions that can be adequately responded to on a troubles-oriented basis. Typically, the questions won't even be asked. However, sociologists ask questions like these all the time.

What, then, does "the sociological analytical approach" mean? Are we to believe that social structures cause crime? Suppose someone sticks a gun in your face and demands your money. Will your first thought be, *I can see why you're doing this: the institutionalized inequality and oppression rampant in our capitalistic system has driven you to this awful point?* Not likely. And I doubt if any sociologist put into this situation would think like this either. Sociologist or nonsociologist—we'd all call the cops.

Viewpoint of Sociologists and Its Effect on Christians

So what? None of this is pertinent to how sociologists think. To claim that "poverty causes crime," is not to say that criminals are hopeless victims of their social locations; instead, the claim means that crime *rates* vary directly with the extent of poverty. In other words, social conditions associated with poverty (at least in an affluent society like America) are conducive to an elevated crime *rate*. Sociologists who make such claims do not (or at least *should* not) mean that criminals bear no personal responsibility for their acts.

This discussion raises a related question: "If poverty and crime are causally related, then why do some poor people commit crimes while others do not?" Not every poor person is a criminal. In fact, very few are. Why is that?

While I'm not going to answer that question, I do want to point out that this is a troubles-oriented question—one which focuses on individual differences. By contrast, the previous question, "Why is there a higher percentage of poor people in prison than rich people?" is a question centered on a structural issue. A proper analysis will have to focus on the social system and not on particular people within the system. Yet, it is precisely this type of structural analysis that is difficult for conservatives to accept, given their individualistic commitments and perceptions.

This inability (or unwillingness) to conceptualize problems as issues is the main reason why many Christians are threatened by sociological analysis. The discussion of issues opens one up to a critical analysis of existing structures—structures like our capitalistic economy, our adversarial legal system, and our educational institutions.[1] It is these structures which radicals say are biased in favor of the more affluent and powerful groups in our society. By contrast, these are the same structures that conservatives prefer to accept and, if necessary, defend. Sometimes this defense extends to the point of ignoring structural questions altogether, or denying that they are even legitimate questions to ask. Rather than critically examine them and, in so doing, question the individual-as-central sensibility that sustains the system's legitimacy, conservatives tend to turn their analytical gaze onto matters of individual differences—and, in particular, to matters of individual moral character. So, for example, we are regularly told by conservative businessmen that "corporations are no better and no worse than the personnel who fill their boardroom, offices, and assembly lines."[2] In like manner, conservative Christians are fond of repeating the only reliable formula for making the world a better place: "Win more people to Christ." Many American slave owners were devoted Christians—yet their Christianity hardly threatened the struc-

---

1. Keep in mind that my primary concern here is with conservative Christian students. I am not saying that all conservatives everywhere are unable to deal responsibly with structural matters or with issues-oriented arguments. Well-educated conservatives may not like particular sociological arguments because of their ideological implications, not simply because of the analytical style implied by the argument. There are, after all, some ideologically conservative sociologists about, and their structural arguments, presumably, are quite acceptable to other conservatives.

Furthermore, it is clear that conservative Christians do not ignore social problems. Even so, it is also clear that their tendency is to recommend personal solutions to these problems. Evangelicals may talk about crime and abortion, inflation and war, but not usually as social institutions. As one evangelical commentator put it: sin is the cause of all social problems, and "sin is a disease that can be remedied only on an individualistic basis. Individuals cannot be changed by changing society, but society can be changed by changing the hearts of individuals" (quoted in Irving Howard's "Christ and the Libertarians," p. 10).

Remember also that the definition of *conservative* I am using here is of the libertarian/individualist variety, rather than the organic/holistic variety.

2. This quote is taken from a chapel address given at Houghton College by Gareth W. Larder, titled "The Social Responsibility of Business," October 22, 1986. In my experience at conservative Christian colleges, students hear a great many such individualistic claims, rarely hearing structurally oriented counter-arguments.

tures of slavery. If anything, it sustained slavery. Even so, observations like these do not appear to lessen enthusiasm for an exclusively troubles-oriented analytical approach amongst modern evangelicals.

In short, for ideological reasons, evangelicals are usually more comfortable around troubles than issues. They tend, therefore, to be uncomfortable whenever the sociological imagination is exercised. The individualistic orientations of conservative Christians function to divert critical attention away from the dominant economic and political structures of society. As a result, "Christian reform" efforts—to the degree that they exist today within conservative Christian churches—tend to focus on the victims of social structures (that is, the poor, the unemployed, the sick) rather than on the structures that produce the victimization.

As David Moberg (1977) observes:

> One of the greatest barriers to active social involvement is the belief that the basic causes of all social problems reside exclusively in individual persons, usually the victims. This is a strongly ingrained characteristic of American intellectual history, so it is not surprising that Christians conform to the perspective of their socio-cultural environment (p. 89).

True, Christians will, for biblical reasons, insist on raising questions about personal morality, but this interest makes them orthodox, not necessarily conservative. There is nothing in orthodox Christian beliefs which hinders an issues-oriented analytical approach. Orthodox Christians who read the Bible carefully recognize that its writers often engaged in analyses of social structures. For example, writers in both the Old and New Testaments generally (in fact, overwhelmingly) account for poverty in terms of unjust laws, exploitative business practices, and other unfair advantages built right into the framework of society. Conservative Christians may like to overlook this fact, or somehow explain it away, but an issues-oriented approach to sin is nevertheless present throughout the Bible (Mott, 1982; Sider, 1977). In fact, it takes an exegetical tour de force to make it come out any other way.

We need to sort out these complex questions in order to understand how orthodox Christianity and the sociological imagination interrelate. Christian writers who ignore structural issues as they analyze social problems, restricting their focus to so-called conspiracies and/or various moral failures of individuals, shortchange their readers.

It is presently popular among many such writers to castigate secular humanists for their presumed conspiratorial efforts to undermine America's moral foundation. Whatever else can be said for or against this thesis, it is perfectly suited to conservative tastes; there is no mention here of the subtle disruption of community ties caused by industrialization, or of technology and the growth of a complex division of labor. All we hear about is a mysterious group of secularists who—for whatever reasons—seeks to erode America's spiritual heritage (cf. LaHaye, 1980).

Good and Bad; Right and Wrong

Many conservative Christian analysts flatly deny that our social problems are at all structural in nature. Typical is the claim that structural changes, proposed as solutions to social problems, "cannot transform bad men into good men."[3]

What are we to make of such claims? First of all, they are difficult to evaluate because the terms are so vague. In this case, we need to know how the analyst defines the words *good* and *bad*. If, by designating some people as "good," the analyst means that these are people who do things that have good consequences (as in "good deeds"), then the analyst is simply incorrect. The rate of doing good deeds *can* be structurally induced, as research like Latane's and Rodin's lady-in-distress experiment clearly demonstrates. By socially engineering a situation, one can easily increase (or decrease) the rate of helping behavior. In the

---

3. This quote is taken from an essay by Carl Henry entitled "Evangelicals in the Social Struggle," *Christianity Today*, 8 Oct. 1956, 10. Henry's position may have changed since then, but this particular quote is used only as a statement representing the core of contemporary evangelical social ethics.

For an extended analysis of evangelical social ethics and the emphasis placed on individualism as illustrated in the pages of *Christianity Today*, compare with Dennis P. Hollinger, *Individualism and Social Ethics*.

case of the lady-in-distress experiment, to raise significantly the percentage of people willing to help, all we need is to place fewer people in the room.

However, deeds are a shaky basis for classifying a person as either good or bad. First of all, the good/bad classification suggests a rather unrealistic dichotomy. After all, no one performs good deeds all the time, nor is everything a person does equally good (or bad). Second, it would usually be a mistake to classify an act morally purely on the basis of its consequences. For example, a person may wish me harm by pushing me to the ground. But what if, by pushing me down, I was unintentionally saved from being hit by an on-rushing car? Was the shove actually a good deed after all—and, if so, should we conclude that the person is really a *good* person after all? Not necessarily.

A distinction must therefore be made between one's moral *intent* and the practical *outcome* of one's action. To distinguish between these two, I will characterize moral intent as, to some degree, *good* or *bad,* whereas outcomes will be characterized as, to some degree, *right* or *wrong.* For example, from a Christian ethical perspective, the person who pushed me out of the car's path had bad intentions, but the act also brought about right consequences.

Christian sociologists routinely need to make these distinctions, analyzing human action in terms of both moral intent and benevolence of outcome. Purely structural adjustments can reduce wrong outcomes (by reducing the rate of crime or the probability of suicide, and so forth) but we also have to inquire into the effects such adjustments can have on moral intent.

Considering the research we reviewed, it would be incorrect to conclude, as some conservatives do, that structural changes cannot "transform bad men into good men." Changes in institutional action can serve as new social contexts (that is, plausibility structures), consequently reshaping the consciousness, including the moral intent, of societal members. For example, by adding a second student to the experimental situation, Latane and Rodin decreased the probability that students would come to the aid of the lady in distress. Apparently, not only right consequences (that is, helping the victim) but also good intentions (as in, wanting to help) were decreased. Even personal motivation can be socially engineered to some degree.

It is possible, however, to bring about structural changes that do not affect moral intent at all. In order to understand how this process works, one must first understand that social structures have both manifest (intended, acknowledged) and latent (i.e., unintended, unacknowledged) effects. For example, the manifest effect of increasing the minimum wage is to increase the income of unskilled workers. The latent effect, however, is to increase the rate of unemployment—since increases in the minimum wage often encourage employers to buy labor-saving devices in an attempt to reduce labor costs, resulting in fewer jobs for the unskilled, young, and the elderly.

From a left-of-center ideological standpoint, legislation that raises the minimum wage may sometimes be a *good* policy, but it may also be the *wrong* policy. To categorize this legislation as "a good thing" is—from a radical position—inconsistent; after all, why would a radical want to increase the unemployment rate?

Because they inappropriately translate *right* and *wrong* into *good* and *bad,* and because they tend to reduce structural issues to personal troubles, conservative Christian reductionists appear to advocate empirically unsound positions. Structural changes *can* produce both good consequences and good intentions, as evaluated from the standpoint of Christian ethical principles. To refuse this conclusion is to turn one's back on the weight of social scientific evidence. Structural changes *can* "transform bad men into good men." Restructured situations can even influence how people think, for example, whether they "feel like" going to the aid of an injured person (or whether doing so makes sense).

The same process applies to other problems, like crime, racial prejudice, alienation, familial instability, unemployment, intergroup hostility, and suicide. Each of these problems is, from a Christian standpoint, a bad thing, yet each of them can be, in certain respects, analyzed (as well as affected) without considering individual moral character.

However, arguing in this way is not to say that these problems are essentially amoral in nature, or that an individual's moral character has nothing to do with hostile, criminal, or suicidal behavior. There's nothing either wrong or incorrect with troubles-oriented analysis *per se.* However, when a troubles-orientation is used exclusively (as it often is within conservative

Christian circles), it provides an inadequate analytical basis with which to explain social action. I have further argued that evangelical Christians have a particular attachment to a reductionistic view of the world—for reasons that have lots to do with their conservatism and little to do with their orthodoxy.

Amoral Structuralism

A related problem, characteristic of contemporary sociologists, mirrors the error of conservative Christians by going to the opposite extreme. Whereas many conservative Christians reduce the analysis of social problems to the moral character of individuals, some structuralist sociologists seem to eliminate the moral dimension altogether.

When sociologists critically analyze the nature of social reality, some of them assume that individual differences (especially moral differences) are irrelevant. At least they often write as if they think individual differences are irrelevant. Of course, in one sense we would expect this from a discipline that tries to be empirical. However, here we seem to encounter the same confusion between morés and morals that we discussed in chapter 2. It is one thing to demonstrate the empirical truth or falsity of a value (something which cannot be done scientifically); it is quite another thing to exclude all references to values in one's sociological analysis, thus ignoring (and thereby implicitly denying) the crucial role that personal moral outlook plays in organizing social action.

As I said, some contemporary sociologists write as if questions of morality are irrelevant to their research. The impression often generated by their writings is that society represents a system of interrelated structures operating in such a mechanistic way that the moral perspectives of members have little or nothing to do with why people think and act as they do.

In some cases, such researchers are guided by certain general (and usually unstated) humanitarian or humanistic values. They often approach analytical problems as if nothing more were involved than figuring out which "structural rearrangement" will bring about the desired result: a reduction in crime, greater access to educational resources for minority groups, more equality in the distribution of scarce goods, and so forth.

The object is to engineer the appropriate social structures in such a way that the desired behavioral change will result. In effect, to borrow a line from T. S. Eliot, these sociologists seem to be searching for "systems so perfect no one will need to be good." I refer to this perspective underlying the great bulk of contemporary sociological theory as *moral structuralism*. It is so named because sociologists often tend to regard people as "actors," wholly determined by social structures. The image of particular people making personal choices is replaced by the image of "role players" whose behavior is dominated by the institutional context.

These theorists write as if poverty is a condition solely created and maintained by institutionalized patterns (monetary policies, class structures, technological systems of production), not because of personal characteristics and personal choices. In addition, they often write as if social organization is established solely on the basis of power or impersonal interdependence, and not on interpersonal trust and moral agreement.[4]

To assume that individuals passively take on the characteristics of whatever system surrounds them is too simplistic. People are moral beings. They will typically choose their options (however limited they may be) according to how they interpret their situations. True, interpretations are shaped by social context, but people should not be defined as passive agents of social contexts—not by Christian sociologists in any event.

---

4. For example, Randall Collins, a contemporary structuralist, approvingly summarizes the "naturalistic materialism" of Thomas Hobbes as a thesis preserved in contemporary sociological theory. Collins credits Hobbes with one of the earliest coherent models of social order. In Hobbes's writings, Collins observes in "The Empirical Validity of Conflict Theory":

> . . . the immortal soul and the Kingdom of Heaven are irrelevant in a material world, where worldly power alone rules; morality is reduced to obedience to social conventions, and these in turn are nothing if not upheld by the state. The state is organized violence, and that is its basis for keeping order; laws are upheld only because the state controls violence, and cannot be a basis for it. Material interest in individual self-preservation is the basic drawing force; good and evil are reduced to appetite and aversion—reward and punishment (*Contemporary Sociological Theories*, p. 174).

While this summary is an adequate description of Hobbes's naturalistic materialism, it is an overstated version of what I call contemporary amoral structuralism. Even so, it does rather crudely state the basic model of society that Christian sociologists ought to firmly reject.

Summary

The moralistic reductionism of conservative Christians represents the antithesis of the amoral structuralism offered by many sociologists. Christian sociologists ought to reject both analytical extremes. On the one hand, moralistic reductionism restricts analytical attention to individual differences. By so doing, we avoid inquiry into how systems influence their members. On the other hand, amoral structuralists assume people act like particles of matter—wholly determined by their social contexts. Furthermore, they appear to assume that social organizations can maintain themselves without (or in spite of) a moral basis. This assumption contradicts the biblical understanding of human action as reflecting moral choices, and must—for this reason alone—be rejected. Society *is* a moral enterprise; society cannot be reasonably thought of as solely a set of impersonal structures.

Social action always represents a complex combination of forces, some of them more related to the character of individuals and some of them more related to the structures of society. Structural issues do influence personal troubles, and vice versa. For example, when faced with a dynamic postindustrial social order that needs fewer unskilled, poorly educated workers, such persons often respond by withdrawing from the labor market and thereby becoming apathetic, relying instead on other economic options, some of them illegal. Correspondingly, some governmental responses (like the institution of certain types of welfare policies) tend to increase personal dependence and reduce individual initiative. In this way, the moral character of people most affected by such structural changes can also undergo change. For example, some may become more criminally inclined, even justifying their illegal actions by claiming that "the system keeps me down" (conveniently ignoring the fact that other people caught in the same circumstances do not turn to crime as a solution). Others may become truly lazy, apathetic, or despondent. These adverse personal reactions can, if sufficiently widespread, bring about further adjustments in institutional patterns—new criminal sanctions or welfare policies, for example—which can then have further effects on individual choices. Thus, a cycle linking issues with troubles is established.

Any analysis that concentrates exclusively on one analytical part without incorporating the other will, of necessity, be seriously impaired. Christian sociologists need to recognize the contributions that both troubles and issue orientations can make to the study of social systems, when combined into a balanced synthesis.

Having said this, however, we have yet to address the ways sociological analysis and Christian faith can complement each other. Despite all the differences and tensions explored in this book, I think the two can be combined to yield a perspective that is as vital as it is rarely encountered. This combination is the subject of the final chapter.

Conclusion
Reflexive Praxis
and Christian Sociology

Christian sociology" does not offer a unique theoretical explanation for social reality; rather, it offers a unique method of approaching social reality. Explanations Christian sociologists offer for empirical phenomena stem from pretty much the same theoretic base shared by non-Christian sociologists. Of course, as I indicated in chapter 2, there are certain philosophical and ideological biases at work in the selection of a theoretical base by Christian sociologists. Even so, theory isn't the key to understanding what the combination of Christianity and sociology has to offer.

Christian sociology is a way of looking at social reality. Actually, it is a combination or integration of several ways. The combination of Christianity and sociology provides a special method for encountering the social world. Through this method we can obtain both a unique way of seeing reality and also a way of learning about reality. In this final chapter we will consider how to see and learn about society from a Christian sociological perspective: we will consider reflexivity as a way of seeing and praxis as a way of learning.

Through Christian conversion and the study of sociology we relearn how to look at the world. Both perspectives involve a set of disciplines—disciplines which allow us to choose analytical options not previously available. In part, these options and the corresponding freedoms they allow become available because we can now see what we could not see before.

The old hymn "Amazing Grace" ably expresses the freedom to be found in Christian conversion:

> I once was lost
>   but now am found,
> Was blind
>   but now I see.

Likewise, there is a freedom found in adopting the sociological perspective. A crucial part of this perspective, as mentioned earlier, is what Mills called "the sociological imagination." This is the willingness and ability to analytically link biography to history. In so doing, we can make analytical connections between parts of our lives not previously seen as connected. We can see, for example, how the ways we earn an income, decorate our homes, raise our children, and think of and worship God, all fall into general patterns, and how these patterns are linked to certain social factors, such as the extent of our education, how much money we earn, and so forth.

Thus, there is a set of disciplines and corresponding freedoms involved in both Christianity and sociology. But freedom in one area may mean bondage in another. Freedom to see *B* clearly may be associated with the inability to see *A*. An early twentieth-century economist and sociologist, Thorstein Veblen, coined the phrase "trained incapacity," referring to the fact that learning can simultaneously open and close perception and understanding.

In short, as we learn to look at things one way, we may develop a trained incapacity to see in other ways. In spite of the freedoms available from Christian and sociological vision, both can (and often do) close down options—options associated with the other perspective. When individuals become Christians, they quite often turn away from the type of skeptical and analytical thinking characteristic of sociologists. The opposite tendency is at least as common. Consequently, the possibility of looking both ways is greatly reduced.

Synthesis via Reflexivity and Praxis

We must learn more about at least two factors in order to overcome trained incapacities that plague the effort to combine Christian and sociological thought. It goes without saying that we begin by learning more about both perspectives, thus opening up options to look both ways. The most important skill resulting from a combination of Christian and sociological perspectives is the ability (coupled with the willingness) to escape the parochial confines each perspective tends to engender when isolated from the other. In other words, one of the most important ways sociology and Christianity can be useful in combination is by generating a cognitive detachment from conventional social reality. I will talk about this detachment in terms of *reflexivity*.

But cognitive detachment, by itself, is not enough. We also need to apply it for the purpose of active involvement in bringing about social change. In short, we need to move from abstract learning for its own sake, to *praxis*—that is, learning through committed involvement. I will argue that both Christianity and sociology have long traditions of defining learning in precisely this way—not as abstracted knowledge but as faithful commitment.

By combining the reflexivity and praxis of both perspectives, we can diminish trained incapacity, combining the two in an analytical perspective more insightful than can be produced when each perspective operates separately.

A Review

As we have seen, Christianity and sociology do not blend into a neatly integrated system. Instead, so-called Christian sociology seems to be a contradiction in terms. Consequently, for Christians to move into sociological quarters, they will first have to rearrange quite a bit of furniture.[1]

---

1. The opposite imagery, that is, of sociology moving into Christian quarters, is not my principal concern here.

I argued in Part 1 that Christianity needs to rehabilitate aspects of contemporary sociological thought. For example, Christians cannot accept at face value the relativity of secular constructionist sociology. Likewise, in Part 2, I discussed how the determinism of structuralist sociology has to be substantially modified, combining its capacity to analyze social systems with a perspective allowing for the possibility of human creativity and moral choice.

There are challenges sociological scholarship can bring to our conceptions of Christianity as well; the analytical and ideological outlook of many Christians is inevitably challenged in the process of settling into sociological accommodations. In particular, the troubles-orientation of American conservatives, long since grafted onto evangelical Christianity, ought to be greatly modified with respect to the issues-oriented perspective of sociology.

Given the challenges—some of them complex and perplexing—of combining science with religion, we could ask why Christians should be interested in combining the insights of sociology with their religious faith. Why not just keep the two separated in their own cognitive compartments? My answer stems from the assumption that, in spite of (and in some important respects, because of) tensions and dilemmas, the combination of sociology and Christianity can have a beneficial effect on both.

Reification and Reflexivity

My argument for Christian sociology will begin by focusing on the concepts of *reification* and *reflexivity*. We will consider them in this order for two reasons. First, reflexivity cannot be properly understood without first understanding the process of reification. Second, reification represents a problem for which reflexivity is the solution.

The basis of the discussion that follows is the sociological insight that, whatever else Christianity is, it is a social institution. This means, as I've stressed before, that the Christian religion is a human construction and hence can be studied as other social institutions—with the full force of sociological skepticism and relativity.

Christianity is an organized religion, complete with denominational structures, creeds, and customs—all of them replete with various (often contradictory) interpretations associated with the respective social locations of the Christian groups committed to them. Of course, sociologists don't have any problems in accounting for these variations. They are well prepared for the fact that rich and poor, black and white, southerner and northerner all have different conceptions of religious reality. They variously interpret everything else; why should religion be any different?

As I have said before, when confronted with the debunking that sociologists are capable of hurling at Christianity, Christians often recoil in fright. Need they do so?

Well, according to orthodox Christians, humanity is "fallen," and all human creation is susceptible to the corrupting effects of sin. This corruption is as applicable to the Christian religion as it is for all the other parts of society—its economy, family forms, legal code, its other religions, and so forth. Despite the fact that Christianity is the institutionalized response to what Christians regard as God's truth, it remains a social institution. As such, it is not exempt from the skepticism with which Christians regard all social institutions. We need to remind ourselves that it is God we worship, and not the Christian religion.

What Is Reification?

We reify the meanings of cultural symbols when these meanings are accepted without question, that is, when they are accepted as givens and the symbols are granted an "inevitable" and "natural" quality. Our lives are full of such givens. Standing a prescribed distance from those with whom we talk, using a certain vocabulary, speaking with an accent, taking so many showers per week, or wearing certain types and styles of clothing are ordinarily unquestioned routines of life. When we come to accept unquestionably these and other ways of thinking and acting, we tend to regard them as universal and immutable. In this way, cultural symbols and their meanings are accepted as more than just *normal* ways of thinking and acting; they are also seen as *natural*. Consequently, other cultures which present to us unfamiliar options (for instance, standing, talking, cleaning, or dressing differently) are seen as "unnatural," not merely as "abnormal."

The process whereby cultural symbols are taken as givens— as natural and thus inevitable—is called "reification." Closely related to reification are processes which we already considered in chapter 2: the restricted outlook which results from reification is called "parochialism"; and the tendency to devalue unfamiliar cultural alternatives is called "ethnocentrism."

There is, however, another side to the coin—for that which has been reified can also be *de*-reified. Without using either term, Linton (1936) describes both sides as follows:

> It has been said that the last thing which a dweller in the deep sea would discover would be water. He would become conscious of its existence only if some accident brought him to the surface and introduced him to air. Man, throughout most of his history, has been only vaguely aware of the existence of culture. The ability to see the culture of one's own society as a whole calls for a degree of objectivity which is rarely, if ever, achieved (p. 88).

This sort of rarely achieved awareness can be (but isn't necessarily) a consequence of the sociological perspective. As Linton notes, it is a quality of awareness that few people achieve—a cognitive detachment from what others regard as natural. In this sense, the objectivity of a dereified perspective represents a quality of analytical detachment from all cultural symbols. At the very least, this sort of objectivity means seeing social reality for what it is: a humanly constructed product. Seen in this way, what was once immutable (let's symbolize it as **REALITY!**) now becomes something tentative and finite ("reality")—which means it is now recognized as a tentative version among many plausible alternatives.

Evidences of reification are usually decried by most sociologists.[2] The reason is straightforward; if we are able to see

---

2. I should say that *certain types* of reification are decried by sociologists. The so-called structuralist sociologists discussed in the last chapter often do well at contributing to the sum total of reification by talking about "roles" and "institutions" as if they are entities in themselves—that is, structures that exist independent of human consciousness. In previous chapters, I have argued that such structures are a product of social interaction and that they shape personal experience and our definitions of reality. They do, but they are not things-in-themselves, independent of humanity and human consciousness. The institution of the family, for example, influences me, and yet it consists of people like me in interaction with each other, creating symbols as they proceed through time.

alternative realities as but mirror images of our own, then we in effect deny that social reality is humanly constructed (and hence variable). Since the recognition that social reality is socially defined and maintained is central to the sociological perspective, the denial tends to close down sociological analysis. This is why sociologists do more than carefully scrutinize expressions of parochialism, such as are found in ethnocentric remarks: they also regard them as ethically undesirable. This is the same reason why so many secular sociologists are often hostile to expressions of Christian commitment—because these commitments imply exclusivistic claims that are the epitome of parochialism (Lehman, 1974).

Sociologists prefer a cosmopolitan outlook—one that allows for "mental mobility"—one capable of easily shifting from one "reality" to another. If we are cosmopolitan in this sense, we willingly acknowledge new ways of thinking and doing things, inquiring how our cultural experiences compare with others.[3] From this cosmopolitan orientation springs cultural relativity (discussed in chapter 3), that is, the willingness to acknowledge alternative, equally plausible ways of defining reality.

For example, sociological cosmopolitans are willing to adopt (but not necessarily to accept) the perspective of both feminists and traditionalists on the subject of marital roles. This sort of cognitive openness presumably extends to all areas of social reality. Sociologists who espouse a cosmopolitan outlook will be equally ready to acknowledge opposing viewpoints, say, the views of those who advocate abortion on demand, on the one hand, and those of anti-abortionists on the other. Both perspectives will be taken as equally viable (but not necessarily as equally valid) ways of defining reality. Of course, sociologists will have personal convictions on these and other matters, but

---

3. Of course, the claimed cosmopolitanism of sociology may sometimes operate so as to close down one's perspective. The assumptions of sociology—its secularist and humanistic starting points, among others—may be (and often are) accepted as givens. As such, it is easier to dismiss alternative perspectives with a cynical guffaw. In this way, the perspective of the sociologist can be every bit as reified and hence unexamined as any Christian perspective. As E. Burke Rochford observes in *Hare Krishna in America:* "Social scientists . . . are often readily able to find the inconsistencies in the behavior of others, yet often remain virtually blind to the inconsistencies in their own lives or in the causes they support" (p. 212).

their hope is that these personal convictions will not stifle their willingness to listen well and to observe carefully.[4]

Even so, sociological cosmopolitanism can sometimes go too far. Total cognitive openness (if such can be even imagined) is indistinguishable from blindness: seeing through everything is the same as seeing through to nothing. Replacing a totally reified world with a totally dereified world is not much of a bargain; it amounts to swapping anomie for alienation. Personally, I'd prefer to have less of both.

Cosmopolitanism is also limited by the nature of scientific research and theory construction. Sociologists cannot equally adopt all perspectives because theory construction requires that they make and apply certain philosophical choices. For example, some sort of perspective on the nature of human nature, the nature of social order, and so forth, will have to be incorporated into sociological theory—knowingly or not. We can't agree with every position simultaneously. Christians will, of course, seek out biblically-based assumptions. As such, their choices will involve parochial interpretations, but then, so will any other set of assumptions incorporated into sociological theory, regardless of how secular and scientific they may be.

Apart from these considerations, the sociological perspective generally works to undermine reified and hence parochial definitions of reality. For this reason, reification, with its resultant parochial outlook, is generally unbecoming to a sociologist.

Reification and Christianity

Reification is equally unbecoming to Christians. I base this conclusion on the response Christ gave to the religious reifications he encountered. Jesus routinely decried Jewish parochialism. In Luke, chapter 4, for example, we read that Jesus was forcefully rejected by his own hometown neighbors. In fact, they tried to kill him. Why? Because Jesus recounted for them the following:

---

4. At this point, the reader needs to keep in mind the discussion of values and science given in chapter 2, particularly the claim that the truth of values cannot be empirically established and the claim that all scientific theory is based on untestable value claims.

"I assure you that there were many widows in Israel in Elijah's time, when the sky was shut for three and a half years and there was a severe famine throughout the land. Yet Elijah was not sent to any of them, but to a widow in Zarephath in the region of Sidon. And there were many in Israel with leprosy in the time of Elisha the prophet, yet not one of them was cleansed—only Naaman the Syrian" (vv. 25-27).

Here Jesus refers to the Old Testament accounts of two Gentiles whose needs were met by God. In so doing, Jesus declared that the Jews were not the center of the universe (as these people apparently thought), and that God cares for Gentiles too. In fact, according to Jesus, Gentiles are sometimes given preference over Jews.

Needless to say, that's not what the Jews wanted to hear. When they heard Jesus speak this way, his neighbors did what ethnocentric people usually do when their reified world is challenged:

All the people in the synagogue were furious. . . . They got up, drove him out of the town, and took him to the brow of the hill on which the town was built in order to throw him down the cliff (vv. 28-30).

To repeat, anything that can be reified can also be dereified. The person who sees the world in dereified terms regards reality as fabricated and thus tentative. However, this awareness doesn't mean that a dereified world is necessarily devalued. Acceptance of the human constructedness of social institutions is not an adequate basis for their rejection. Both slavery and monogamy have been important parts of American society, and as such, both have been humanly constructed (and reconstructed). Of course, we now reject one and accept the other, but this differential response does not alter the human origins of either.

Nor for the Christian does the acceptance of monogamy as a humanly constructed institution reduce it to merely an arbitrary (and thus easily discarded) social form. We can and should accept the family as divinely sanctioned and monogamy as a useful cultural form—as an historical product of human interaction and definition. (New Testament writers generally endorse monogamy, but it is not prescribed anywhere. Elders are supposed to be the husbands of one wife, but that's about it. Marital fidelity is commanded, but not monogamy.)

The same can be said of the Christian church. All churches represent human constructions, based on various interpretations, growing out of different cultural traditions and historical experiences. Even if this much is granted, Christians usually won't leave the matter there: to the notion that churches are human constructions they add the belief that the Holy Spirit provides divine guidance to Christ's church. Without this faith, the church is reduced to the status of any other arbitrarily constructed social institution (which is exactly what secular sociologists think it is).

Christian sociologists need to tread the slippery middle ground between an all-embracing cynicism so common among secular scholars ("Claims of knowing God's truth are dangerous delusions") and heretical omniscience so common among conservative Christians ("Our understanding is identical to God's truth").

Dereification is promoted not by cynicism but by a skepticism characteristic of certain brands of Christianity. The skeptical tone of sectarian Christianity (considerably muted in the more affluent denominations) is engendered by its skeptical view of the *cosmos*—the world that we Christians are presumably "just a-passin' through." Bible writers warn repeatedly that, even though God so loved the *cosmos* that he gave his only Son for it, it can nevertheless be an evil trap. Those who become overly involved in its principles and procedures can be ensnared by its subtle influences. Christians who take this message seriously are less likely to reify the ways of the *cosmos*.

Christian skepticism is born of a detachment expressed in terms like *sojourner* and *pilgrim*. Peter describes the followers of Christ as "a chosen people, . . . a people belonging to God, . . . called . . . out of darkness into his wonderful light" (1 Peter 2:9). Christians are called "aliens and strangers in the [*cosmos*]" . . . (v. 11).

Such marginality is engendered by certain Christian doctrines, among them beliefs in the depravity of humanity and the omniscience of God.

Certain forms of both Christianity and sociology can serve as invitations to cognitive detachment and openness, a willingness to be marginal and thus open to other possibilities. The combination of the two can be truly liberating. Christian sociologists ought to be marginal to all cultural perspectives—the ones that are familiar and personally espoused (including all the Christian ways of thinking and doing), as well as those that are unfamiliar (and perhaps even abhorrent).

What I am advocating, however, is a rare blend. Christianity has often served opposite ends.

Parochialism and Christianity

Like adherents to other universal religions, orthodox Christians claim absolute and final truth. By doing so, they often fall into a trap—one which ironically conflicts with the very truth they claim to know: they become arrogant in their "possession" of exclusive truth. In doing so, they negate the humility and meekness that Christ said ought to characterize the lives of his followers. Absolutism, exclusivity, parochialism, confrontation of error, arrogance, self-contradiction: these are persistent problems for orthodox Christians.

The claim of exclusive truth can, of course, serve useful ideological purposes. Exclusive claims to truth can be quite useful to those who need to bolster their convictions about what is in their interests to believe. Thus, Christian monarchs once claimed the divine right to rule; American plantation owners claimed a God-given right to own slaves; and countless nations have claimed God's exclusive support for their wars against each other. From the Crusades and the various inquisitions, to modern-day Christian "segregation academies," espousal of traditional Christianity has often served the narrow interests of powerful groups who prefer to think that the expedient way is also the moral way.

But it doesn't have to be this way. Christianity can also serve the cause of dereification, cosmopolitanism, and cultural challenge. The most recent reminders of this capability include the civil rights movement, led in large part by Christian clergy (few of them evangelicals) who based their unwillingness to obey the dictates of legal segregation on their commitment to what they called "God's higher law." It should not be particularly surprising that other movements challenging the status quo (for instance, abolition, women's rights, temperance, and anti-abortion) have also been sponsored to varying degrees by these same Christian commitments.

After all, consider the source. Christ shocked the Jewish traditionalists by repeatedly saying, "It is written, but I say unto you. . . ." What's more, Christ associated with notorious deviants, regularly denounced the powerful segments of Jewish society, and broke all sorts of ethnic, religious, and social taboos. He did all this with the obvious intent of demonstrating that by creating a reified religious tradition, the religious leaders had turned away from God's truth and love and were serving instead their own narrow, parochial interests.

Decrying the bondage of reified traditional religion, Christ declared truth as a liberating force. The truth he exemplified came not in the form of exclusivistic doctrines but in obedience to God's law and in love for others. *People will know my disciples,* Christ said, *by the love they have for each other.* He would know who his true followers were by their commitment to God's law—the command to love God and to treat others as we would have them treat us.

Christianity continues to liberate from the conventions of the *cosmos*—encouraging the establishment of communal relations in a grossly impersonal society, calling us to renounce materialism in the midst of the world's most materialistic culture, and breaking down social exclusivities through the power of common grace bestowed equally on all.

Such liberation cannot result from "easy believism." Christian dogma is not some sort of magical force that overcomes all the anti-Christian influences of the *cosmos* simply by being believed. Although contemporary evangelicals often seem fixated on it, correct belief is never enough. In fact, it is often a snare.

It is faith, Bible writers declare, which is the true center of God's salvation plan. Faith combines belief with a willingness to personally experience the truth and be ruled by it.

Beyond Dereification to Reflexivity

Contacting and claiming God's truth is not simply a matter of dereifying the *cosmos*. By acknowledging and claiming the truth of the gospel, the Christian stands apart from the *cosmos* and critiques it from a transcendent moral standpoint. When released from parochial interests, the power of the gospel can encourage us to be a truly peculiar people. So it is that Christ claimed his kingdom was not part of the *cosmos;* so it is that Paul claimed to be a person "set apart" for God's unique purposes (Rom. 1:1).

Included in the role of being Christ's disciples is the capacity to stand outside the *cosmos* and look at it as outsiders do. The result is the ability to see culture and social location as a coincidence. It is a cognitive capability related to what sociologists call "marginality." This is where Christian sociologists need to be: on the experiential and cognitive margins of conventional life; familiar with other perspectives, and, as a result, taking none of them (including their own) for granted. It goes without saying, then, that Christian sociologists have a double incentive to become marginal people. The result of such marginality ought to be an uncommon *reflexivity.*

To be reflexive is to be self-reflective—that is, self-aware. But true reflexivity goes far beyond the willingness and ability to reflect upon oneself and others. It also requires that we be able to stand outside our position—cognitively speaking—and evaluate it from a detached (objective) perspective. Of course, "objectivity" here does not mean "without bias"; rather, it means the capacity to make evaluations on the basis of both theoretical and ethical standards which transcend immediate interests. In other words, reflexive people are committed to standards of thought and action superior to their immediate interests and ideological commitments. It is these standards which direct us, not the other way around. In this sense, reflexivity involves objectivity.

The heart of reflexivity is the capacity for self-criticism—that is, the ability to articulate one's previously reified interpretations, evidential lapses, self-congratulatory rationalizations, logical flaws—and to adjust accordingly. The best biblical illustration of reflexivity I can think of concerns King David. Consider his state of mind just after the prophet Nathan told him the story about the rich man who took and killed the farmer's pet lamb (2 Sam. 11, 12). David was indignant at the rich man's sin and declared that he should die. Nathan pointed at the king and said, "You are the man!"

Instant reflexivity!

The results can be found in Psalm 51:

> Wash away all my iniquity
>   and cleanse me from my sin.
>
> *For I know my transgressions,*
>   *and my sin is always before me.*
> Against you, you only, have I sinned
>   and done what is evil in your sight,
> so that you are proved right when you speak
>   and justified when you judge.
>
> Surely I was sinful at birth,
>   sinful from the time my mother conceived me.
> Surely you desire truth in the inner parts;
>   you teach me wisdom in the inmost place.
>
> Verses 2-6, italics added

Motivation for the Christian to adopt a reflexive perspective springs from the desire to conform to God's law. It begins from the realization that people who know the most about the *cosmos* are least likely to be shaped by it. It is this *cosmos* that Paul warns us against in Romans 12:2, where he writes: "Do not conform any longer to the pattern of this [*cosmos*], but be transformed by the renewing of your mind. Then you will be able to test and approve what God's will is—his good, pleasing, and perfect will."

The reflexivity of the Christian sociologist is fostered by the capacity to see "reality" as a socially constructed product, to gain thereby a measure of detachment from it, and hence a measure of control over it. We cannot progress in reformulating "social reality" in obedience to the command to become part of the kingdom of God if we cannot detach ourselves sufficiently from the *cosmos* to critique it on the basis of both sociological theory and biblical values.

Racism and Christianity

To cite one historical example, consider racism in America. This social ideology declared that blacks really are (1) a distinguishable and entirely separate group; and (2) an inferior race vis-à-vis whites. No matter that both of these ideas were fictions with no other basis—scientific or otherwise; the fact is, they were believed, and were reified—taken as givens, immutable features of the natural world and part of the fixed order of things. Some people still define reality this way.

Racism was formulated as a defense of both slavery and the system of racial segregation eventually replacing it. The key feature of this development, however, was that racism grew alongside both Christianity and democracy. How ironic—that the systematic and legal subordination of a group could be adopted in a society where the Christian gospel and the idea that "all men are created equal" were so widely believed!

To begin with, it was in the economic interest of powerful groups to establish and maintain slavery as a form of trade and cheap labor. Over a long period of time, an ideology was formed whereby an entire way of life established around slavery was legitimated. White supremacy was justified in the face of democracy and Christianity by means of an ideology that reduced to the following syllogism:

All humans are created equal (a democratic and, some think, Christian principle)

Slaves are not equal (an obvious fact, given the slave laws)

All slaves are Negroes (another obvious fact)

_____

Therefore: Negroes are not human (a central racist belief)

This syllogism may not represent flawless logic, nor was it always (or even usually) argued out in explicit form like this, but the conclusion was nonetheless drawn. It had (and still has) powerful effects on American culture and society (Jordan, 1969).

Although it represented a most unlikely combination of beliefs and values, slavery, democracy, and Christianity comfortably co-existed for several hundred years. Such can be the power of economic interests even in the face of political and religious ideals.

Racists claim that blacks deserve to be degraded and exploited because of their presumed inherent inferiority. The ideology of racism is a perspective of hate. Can a person be a racist and still be a follower of Jesus Christ?

From our perspective as twentieth-century citizens, most of us would argue that racial identity cannot legitimately be a basis for discrimination. Most Christians now believe that we are equal in our common sinfulness, and that we are made equal by divine grace given to all who will receive it. Moreover, Christians believe that we should not oppress others, but love them even if they are our enemies. We should believe all this—and act as if we do.

Over the course of our history, a lot of self-proclaimed Christians did not believe these things (or, if they did, they didn't act as if they did). Note first of all that the American South has often been referred to as "the Bible Belt," for good reason. Racism and Christianity co-existed, and even flourished together there for hundreds of years. The point is clear: the gospel has often been subordinated to the interests of powerful groups. More to the point here, the influence of these interests grows to the extent that the resulting ideologies are reified.

Look what happened with American slavery and Christianity; many slave owners declared themselves pious Christians. Yet the brutal racist system they supported contradicted the most rudimentary Christian claims. As important as they often are, sincerity and zealousness are not the keys to "victorious Christian living." Rather, the key is marginality to the *cosmos* coupled with the willingness and capacity to understand and obey Christ's gospel.

This process of reinterpreting the gospel to suit the *cosmos* has not ended with the end of slavery. A similar process can be seen among modern Christians who have sold out to contemporary values, such as materialism and hedonism. John White [1979] observes that contemporary Christians are:

> . . . often, like sponges, soaked to capacity with the value system of the society we live in . . . [for] we have overvalued material prosperity and have underestimated, taken for granted, or even forgotten the God of power and love we profess to worship. We claim to have faith in Him. But so long as we are harassed by anxiety about our financial security or overly impressed by the

importance of money in Christian work, our profession is hollow
and our footsteps follow in the pathway to whoredom (p. 76).

To a greater extent than most Christians like to admit, we
have been co-opted by the *cosmos*. Consequently, we need the
discernment necessary to see that Christianity is an integral
part of the *cosmos*. Sociology can help us here. When we turn the
skeptical eye of sociology onto evangelicalism, for example, we
can see more clearly how it has co-opted (or has been co-opted
by) aspects of its social milieu, which is middle-class and mid-
twentieth century American. We'll call it "middle-American."

Consistent with its social location, evangelicalism has become imbued with a number of cultural traits that aren't the
least bit biblical, but are solidly middle-American—among
them being urges to quantify, promote the individual, and reach
quick-fix solutions (Miller, 1986). In measuring "success," a
technologically advanced culture tends to substitute quantity
for quality. Everything from who we think we are as a nation
("the most productive nation on earth") to who we think we are
as persons (as assessed by scores on various "personality inven-
tories") is subject to quantification. So it is with evangelicals;
the success of our evangelical crusades is measured in terms of
"souls won," and the quality of our churches evaluated in terms
of budget size and church growth. That the Bible defines success
in purely qualitative terms ("love, joy, peace") seems to matter
little.

In our promotion of individualism we have concentrated on
saving the individual *from* eternal damnation, but we have not
concentrated on what the individual is saved *to*. Our image of
God's church is that of a collection of saved souls—a whole no
greater than the sum of its parts. The church does not represent
an alternative social system; it is for the most part a clone of the
middle-American style itself: privatistic, fragmented, materialistic, and rationalized.

In choosing to copy the *cosmos,* we often take the "quick-fix"
approach. Consistent with our social location, we have sim-
plified and rationalized the process of salvation into "spiritual
laws" and discipleship into "steps to the victorious life" (Hunter,
1983). Likewise, evangelicals often assume that social problems
like crime, divorce, and poverty can be solved only if enough

individuals become Christians. Yet, in the face of the exponential growth of American evangelicalism, we are confronted with the even greater growth of these social problems.

If the problem cannot be seen for what it is, then there will be no perceived need for a solution. We Christians need to loosen ourselves from the grip of the middle-America culture. We need the reflexivity both biblical Christianity and sociology can provide—not simply each perspective learned, but both perspectives combined, so that one can act as a challenge for the other, each providing for the other what it cannot provide for itself.

To repeat: the major rationale for Christians studying sociology centers on the hope that the more Christians know about how the *cosmos* operates (to include how it is reified), the more likely they will be able to influence, alter, or avoid its snares. In this case at least, ignorance is not bliss.

Does the sociological perspective advocated here have implications that run counter to what Christianity is all about? That depends on the function Christianity serves. If Christianity is used as an ideological support for the *cosmos,* then a Christian sociological perspective will be perceived as a threat. That's the way it must be. However, if Christianity is defined as a challenge to society—as a radical alternative—sociology can serve Christian ends. *All this comes down to the question of who we say Jesus is.*

Christ and Culture

Whatever else we can say about Jesus, he demonstrated a striking reflexivity. As such, he adopted a perspective that transcended ordinary ideological categories. He drove parochial people crazy. He still does. Parochial people who would follow Jesus either have to redefine him or become less parochial.

In his parables, the good guys became bad guys, and vice versa. He taught that the principles of the *cosmos* are twisted: that discipleship requires that powerful Christians must serve powerless Christians; that his disciples must look out after the welfare of others—even for the welfare of their enemies; that his disciples should lend money freely without expecting it to be repaid; that they should go further than they are asked to go in service to others; they were not to resist those who attacked them; and he said they should expect to be persecuted if and when they obey these commands.

Like other reflexive people, Christ was not restricted by conventional protocol. In fact, he went to extremes in this regard; he hung around beggars, tax collectors, poor people, outcasts, people with communicable diseases, and even a fair number of whores. In fact, he actually seemed to prefer the company of whores to that of certain "respectable people." Whores, it seems, had an integrity Christ appreciated; at least they didn't pretend to be something other than what they were.

Needless to say, Christ didn't always act in "proper" conventional ways. He broke the law, and sometimes he went out of his way to do it right in front of the authorities. Christ apparently had a running feud with those in positions of power. His response to leaders, rich people, and "respectables" was consistent: their power, privilege, and prestige were substantial handicaps to entering the kingdom. Clearly, he loved the people concerned, but at the very least he seriously questioned their social locations and challenged them to revolutionize their lives—to sell all and follow him, to leave everything behind and seek first God's kingdom. No wonder so many people can only *pretend* to be his disciples!

My point here is that Christ did not buy into the *cosmos,* the standard cultural definitions of his day. If we are to be his disciples, we are going to have to become like him.

How *did* Jesus regard "reality"? It is apparent that he regarded it as *questionable* (that is, based on corrupt principles); *tentative* (a lasting reality has yet to be fully realized); and *translucent* (the real reality, which operates on different principles, lies behind this facade that most people take as "real").

Reality as *questionable, tentative,* and *translucent:* this is the type of reality Jesus claimed. Consequently, the Jesus I have been describing is still not too popular. When described in the terms used here, he wouldn't even be recognized in many Christian quarters today. We want to be promised success and personal happiness, which he said his disciples would receive, but not before they denied themselves, picked up their crosses, and followed him. He offered us no easy answers, yet that's the kind we prefer. In response to complex theological and ethical questions, he told obscure parables. (We're still trying to figure out what some of them mean.) He issued difficult commands (telling his followers to hate their parents, to cut off their offending arms, and so forth) so that his disciples cried, "If you keep this up, no one will follow you!"

Those who long for certitude—who claim to know fully the absolute truth—will have little to do with this Jesus. They will have to construct a Jesus more suited to their tastes. And they do. Similarly, these people know that the sociological perspective (with all its debunking and skepticism about "reality") isn't what they want.

On the other hand, those who believe that the key to salvation is faith—consisting of belief in things not seen but still hoped for—will welcome the reflexivity that Christian sociology provides.

Following the advice and warning of Paul in Romans 12, we need to prepare ourselves mentally, so that this humanly made-up conventional order doesn't conform us to its images of what is "natural." Instead, we need to become a peculiar reflexive people, attending to the alternative reality of the gospel.

The bad news is that we are sinners and deserve death. The good news is that God loves us anyway. Because of this, God expects us to act in just and loving ways toward others as a sign of our salvation. We do this by having our minds transformed, to become like Jesus, who was ever ready to suspend belief in the *cosmos*. We must commit ourselves, through faith, to Christ's alternative way of defining what's important and what's not.

However, if we follow this advice, we must not expect parochial people (including parochial Christians) to like it much. They'll probably say that we're the ones with the problem and will insist we need to change our attitude. Even so, we must hold fast to the alternative ethic of Jesus Christ: where down is up, foolishness is wisdom, and their dirge of despair is our song of hope (Kraybill, 1978).

Christian and Sociological Praxis

Earlier, in chapter 4, I argued that the tensions evangelicals have with the search for truth stems from the overemphasis given to correct religious belief. Part of this tension can be traced to the gradual adoption of ancient Greek rationalism into

Christian thought. Plato's idealism, with his assumptions that certitude could be reached by means of abstract reason, continues to be a powerful influence.

The ancient Greeks used the word for knowledge as a *noun*— a goal to be searched for, located, and possessed. In sharp contrast, the ancient Hebrews expressed knowledge as a *verb*—as wisdom espoused by means of active commitment. It is from this source that Christianity drew its inspiration for the concept of *faith:* knowledge of God by means of faithful obedience to divine law, the chief of which is to worship God and love each other.

In this respect, it is instructive to compare the writings of Plato (with his emphasis on logical dichotomies expressed through dialogues which reduce to syllogisms) to that of Jesus Christ, with his call for obedience to the truth expressed in the form of stories. Yet, when it comes to discussions about truth among evangelicals, it seems as if Plato holds the upper hand.

One characteristic of ancient Greek thought was its dualism: they contrasted mind with body, knowledge with action, truth with error, and so forth. Dualism has since become a central feature of Western thinking. It can be found in sociological thought (facts vs. values; empirical vs. normative concerns, and so forth), as well as in Christian thought ("spiritual" vs. "worldly" spheres; propositional vs. relational truth, and so forth).

Such dualism is particularly unfortunate because it obscures (one could say, *distorts*) understanding in both realms. One of the most unfortunate dualisms is the opposition of knowledge to practice. The concept of *praxis* denies this dualism—indeed, suggests that knowledge and practice have reciprocal influences. Here we affirm what otherwise seems so obvious: that knowledge continually shapes experience, and that it is formed and confirmed by that experience.

For Christians, refusal to think in dualistic terms means that faith is not defined as either belief or social action, but is defined instead as committed belief put into proper action. The aim is *shalom*—that is, right relationship—with God, with other humans, and with the rest of creation. *Shalom* cannot be achieved without the integration of belief and committed action.

With this idea in mind, it is easier to understand how the apostle John uses the word *know* in the following passage:

Dear friends, let us love one another, for love comes from God. *Everyone who loves has been born of God and knows God.* Whoever does not love does not know God, because God is love. . . . Dear friends . . . we also ought to love one another (1 John 4:7, 8, 11, italics added).

For Christian sociologists, the rejection of dualism means that theory and application must be integrated. Scientific knowledge is never an end unto itself. We can never be content with the separation of fact and value, or with the pretense that personal values can be meaningfully separated ("bracketed") from one's sociological research. Theoretical language is useful, but it is a preface to the value-committed language of application.

Our need, then, is to be able to integrate empirical observation (fact) with ethical principle (value). I certainly do not wish to suggest that facts and values can be interchanged—only that the two must be *integrated*. Facts without values turn into trivialities. Values without facts threaten to degenerate into mindless (and often dangerous) dogmatism.

To borrow an example from physics, consider the second law of thermodynamics. Given in abstract theoretical language, the law states that energy flows from low-entropic to high-entropic states. Restated, heat cannot of itself pass from a colder to a hotter body; in the natural way of matter, heat can flow only in the opposite direction. The implication is that heat is lost whenever it is converted into energy. One of several meanings of this is that the universe is set up so that there is a finite amount of energy available.

Put bluntly, there no such thing as a free lunch. All energy use is costly in terms of energy loss. What's more, the loss is permanent. If accurate (and if there are no other important qualifications to make), this means that each hot shower we take, each trip we take in a car, each baby born, subtracts from the pool of energy available in the universe.

By restating the law in this way, we have moved from a rhetoric of abstract theory to a rhetoric of praxis. Most importantly, praxis rhetoric begs the inclusion of ethical considerations, and raises all sorts of ethically related questions, such as: what are our obligations to our ecological system—with its finite supply of energy? Is it good to increase the total human population indefinitely? Is an economy based on individual competition and expanding material consumption the wisest policy? Using Christian rhetoric, we could ask, "What are our obligations as stewards of God's earthly kingdom?" By moving toward a praxis orientation in this way, fact meets value, the combination enriches itself, and scientific and religious thinking are explicitly integrated.

Just as theoretical language can be translated into the rhetoric of praxis in physics, so can similar translations be made with the rhetoric of sociological theory. Consider the proposition that a group's ideological position will tend to shift so as to be made compatible with the material and social interests consistent with its goals. In other words, those dominant groups benefitting from a stratification system will tend to be ideologically conservative with respect to that system, as will those subordinate groups which (for whatever reasons) identify with them. Stated more directly, powerful and privileged people generally seek to preserve the social system that helps them come out on top by adopting a style of thinking defending that system as legitimate. Even members of subordinate groups who, for whatever reasons, associate their fate with the system will support it. They will continue to do so, even though it could be shown that they continue to lose because the system operates as it does. Put even more bluntly, interests (including "false" interests) are often more compelling than either evidence or reason.

Implied here is the idea that group interests tend to dominate and shape consciousness. It is relatively easy to be co-opted into thinking in patterns which support our present or hoped-for life circumstances. Stated this way, a warning immediately sounds for Christians: to what degree are we co-opted by our material and social interests? Have Christians compromised the gospel in order to fit more comfortably into the *cosmos*—a system that actually works in some ways to undermine the gospel? In order to find out, would we be willing to (or even able to) alter our social location and hence our interests so as to see our circumstance from a different perspective?

Whatever the answers, the questions are valuable in themselves, for if the questions are not asked, answers will not be sought. We will remain—self-satisfied—in our present circumstances, and in so doing, sell our birthrights cheap. We need to be challenged to actively involve ourselves in altering, if necessary, our own life circumstances so as to observe as best we can the effects such changes have on how we view "reality."

Do conservative Christians tend to take an exclusively individualistic analytical approach? Do conservative Christians tend to identify with the comfortable, the powerful, the respectable? A praxis approach represents a constant encouragement to test out our theories by direct personal involvement—by investing our lives in our knowledge, and vice versa.

Robert Clark (1983), a Christian sociologist who advocates a praxis approach, issues this challenge:

> [P]raxis is an important way to see if we really do understand social life. [We Christian sociologists] have elaborated elegant sounding notions regarding structural evil, fallenness, injustice, idolatry, and so forth. Do our ideas work, fit our experiences in grappling with real struggles? Of what value are our ideas when put into practice? Do we dare test them in the neighborhoods, boardrooms, caucuses, and third world villages? (p. 11)

For the Christian sociologist, abstracted knowledge is never enough. Nor is it enough to say that knowledge must be acted upon. We begin a praxis approach by recognizing that knowledge is both shaped and confirmed by personal experience. This doesn't mean that knowledge is a mere by-product of experience; it *does* mean that knowledge segregated from experience is without validity and value.

The key to benefitting from the combination of sociology and Christianity is in recognizing and experiencing how truth stands the test of careful, skeptical, and actively involved scrutiny. To do so requires that we learn to think and act reflexively.

Summing Up

To the degree that this discussion has been convincing and helpful, the reader is now better able to appreciate the mutual benefits that a dialogue between Christianity and sociology offers. An important consideration: Christians need to have their parochial view of the world—*including* Christianity—challenged by the skeptical orientation of modern sociology. We need to be able to critique in a reflexive way (and jettison if necessary) some of the reified cultural baggage accumulated over the centuries. In particular, the commitment of evangelicals to an unbiblical ideology of individualism indicates the degree to which Christian thinking has been influenced by our cultural context.

In short, we need to incorporate the sociological imagination into the way we understand the gospel, that is, on contemporary evangelical interpretations of the gospel. The desired result is a deeper understanding of how Christians can be *in* but not be *of* the *cosmos*. Of course, by saying this I am not claiming that the sociological perspective is a prerequisite to salvation. I *am* saying that the reflexivity generated by the sociological imagination can be of use in breaking down reification of the sort that hinders a genuine faith response. It is faith in Jesus that saves, not certainty. And not sociology.[5]

By the same token, secular sociology needs to be challenged to acknowledge its empirical limits, and to recognize and examine its implicit metaphysical foundations. If it is true that sociology rests on such assumptions, then Christian sociology can offer a more deliberate, comprehensive, and, I believe, truer perspective than is otherwise encountered within naturalistic sociology.

Because of the tensions inherent in the combination, Christian-informed sociology can be of genuine benefit to those claiming the lordship of Jesus Christ over all their thoughts and actions.

---

5. Admittedly, there are many questions begged in this brief discussion—in particular, questions about the limits of dereification. How far can this process be taken? Pushed to the extreme, do we not end up with anomie and the collapse of all knowledge? On what grounds can Christians claim to reify their view of reality, yet accept this as legitimate? While these questions fall outside the parameters of this book, I have discussed them elsewhere. *See* "Values, Alienation and Christian Sociology." *Christian Scholar's Review*, 15, no. 1:8-27, 1985; *see also* (with Brian Sayers) "Between Alienation and Anomie: The Integration of Sociology and Christianity." *Christian Scholars Review*, 1988.

References

Aronson, Elliot. 1980. *The Social Animal*. San Francisco: Freeman.

Bagby, James W. 1957. "A Cross-Cultural Study of Perceptual Predominance in Binocular Rivalry." *Journal of Abnormal and Social Psychology* 54:331–34.

Bendix, Reinhard. 1971. "Sociology and Ideology." In *The Phenomenon of Sociology*, ed. Edward Tiryakian, 173–87. New York: Appleton-Century-Crofts.

Berger, Peter. 1963. *Invitation to Sociology: A Humanistic Perspective*. Garden City: Doubleday.

Blamires, Harry. 1978. *The Christian Mind*. Ann Arbor: Servant.

Burwell, Ronald. 1981. "On Sleeping with an Elephant: The Uneasy Alliance Between Christian Faith and Sociology." *Christian Scholar's Review* 10:195–203.

Carter, John D., and S. Bruce Narramore. 1979. *The Integration of Psychology and Theology: An Introduction*. Grand Rapids: Zondervan.

Clark, Robert. 1983. "Praxis Makes Perfect: Beyond Conceptual Integration in Sociology." Paper read at the Association of Christians Teaching Sociology, at Eastern College, St. Davids, PA.

179

Collins, Randall. 1978. "The Empirical Validity of Conflict Theory." In *Contemporary Sociological Theories,* ed. Alan Wells. Santa Monica: Goodyear.

———, and Michael Makowsky. 1987. *The Discovery of Society.* New York: Random.

Gaede, Stan. 1985. *Where Gods May Dwell.* Grand Rapids: Zondervan.

———, and Robert Clark. 1981. "Where Your Treasure Is: Explorations in the Sociology of Knowledge." Paper read at annual meeting of the Association of Christians Teaching Sociology, at Calvin College, Grand Rapids, MI.

Greeley, Andrew. 1977. *No Bigger Than Necessary: An Alternative to Socialization, Capitalism, and Anarchism.* New York: Meridian.

Hermann, Kenneth. 1983. Review of *Christianity Challenges the University,* ed. by Peter Wilkes. *Christian Scholar's Review* 12:85–86.

Hillery, George A. 1981. "Freedom, Love, and Community: An Outline of a Theory." In *In Gods We Trust: New Patterns of Religious Pluralism in America,* ed. Thomas Robbins and Dick Anthony, 303–25. New Brunswick: Transaction.

Hollinger, Dennis P. 1984. *Individualism and Social Ethics: An Evangelical Syncretism.* New York: Univ. Press.

Howard, Irving. 1958. "Christ and the Libertarians." *Christianity Today,* 17 March, 10.

Hunter, James. 1983. *American Evangelicalism: Conservative Religion and the Quandary of Modernity.* New Brunswick: Rutgers Univ. Press.

Jordan, Winthrop. 1969. *White Over Black: American Attitudes Towards the Negro, 1550–1812.* Baltimore: Pelican.

Kraybill, Donald. 1978. *The Upside-Down Kingdom.* Scottsdale: Herald.

Kuhn, Thomas. 1970. *The Structure of Scientific Revolutions.* Chicago: University of Chicago Press.

LaHaye, Tim. 1980. *Battle for the Mind.* Old Tappan: Revell.

Latane, Bibb, and Judith Rodin. 1969. "A Lady in Distress: Inhibiting Effects of Friends and Strangers on Bystander Intervention." *The Journal of Experimental Social Psychology* 5:189–202.

Lehman, Edward. 1974. "Academic Discipline and Faculty Religiosity in Secular and Church-Related Colleges." *Journal for the Scientific Study of Religion* 13:205–12.

Lewis, C. S. 1943. *Mere Christianity.* New York: Macmillan.

Lewis, Michael. 1978. *The Culture of Inequality.* New York: Meridian.

Linton, Ralph. 1936. *The Study of Man.* New York: Appleton-Century-Crofts.

Lyon, David. 1975. *Christianity and Sociology.* Downers Grove: Inter-Varsity.

_____. 1982. "Sociology and Humanness: The Action-Structure Tension in Secular and Christian Thought." Paper presented at the annual meeting of the Mid-West Sociological Society, at Des Moines, Iowa.

MacKay, Donald M. 1974. *The Clockwork Image.* Downers Grove: Inter-Varsity.

Miller, Hal. 1986. "The Uneasy Conscience of Modern Evangelicalism." *Voices,* July, 10–12.

Mills, C. Wright. 1959. *The Sociological Imagination.* New York: Oxford University Press.

Moberg, David. 1962. "Christianity and Relativism." *Journal for the American Scientific Affiliation* 14 (June), 34–48.

_____. 1982. "Is There a Christian Sociology?" Tenth Congress, International Sociological Association, Mexico City, Mexico.

_____. 1979. *Spiritual Well-being: Sociological Perspectives.* Washington, D.C., University Press of America.

_____. 1977. *The Great Reversal: Evangelicalism and Social Concern.* Philadelphia: Lippincott.

Mott, Stephen. 1982. *Biblical Ethics and Social Change.* New York: Oxford University Press.

Perkins, Richard. 1985. "Values, Alienation, and Christian Sociology." *Christian Scholar's Review,* 15, no. 1:8–27.

Perkins, Richard, and Brian Sayers. 1988. "Between Alienation and Anomie: The Integration of Sociology and Christianity." *Christian Scholar's Review* (forthcoming).

Poloma, Margaret. 1980. "Theoretical Models of the Person in Contemporary Sociology: Toward Christian Sociological Theory." In *A Reader in Sociology: Christian Perspectives,* ed. Charles P. DeSanto, Calvin Redekop, and William Smith-Hinds, 199–215. Scottsdale: Herald.

Quinney, Richard. 1980. *Providence: The Reconstruction of Social and Moral Order.* New York: Longman.

Reiman, Jeffrey H. 1984. *The Rich Get Richer and the Poor Get Poorer: Ideology, Class, and Criminal Justice.* 2d ed. New York: John Wiley and Sons.

Ritzer, George. 1980. *Sociology: A Multiple Paradigm Science*. Boston: Allyn and Bacon.

Rochford, E. Burke. 1985. *Hare Krishna in America*. New Brunswick: Rutgers University Press.

Ryan, William. 1976. *Blaming the Victim*. Rev. ed. New York: Vintage.

Sider, Ronald. 1977. *Rich Christians in an Age of Hunger: A Biblical Study*. Downers Grove: InterVarsity.

Vidich, Arthur, and S. M. Lyman. 1985. *American Sociology: Worldly Rejections of Religion and Their Directions*. New Haven: Yale University Press.

White, John. 1979. *The Golden Cow: Materialism in the Twentieth Century Church*. Downers Grove: InterVarsity.

Wuthnow, Robert. 1973. "Religious Commitment and Conservatism: In Search of an Illusive Relationship." In *Religion and Sociological Perspective,* ed. Charles Clock. Belmont, CA: Wadsworth.

Index